416

RELEASED

D1257965

BASIC ENGLISH AND ITS USES

Books by
I. A. RICHARDS

PRINCIPLES OF LITERARY CRITICISM

PRACTICAL CRITICISM

MENCIUS ON THE MIND

COLERIDGE ON IMAGINATION

INTERPRETATION IN TEACHING

THE PHILOSOPHY OF RHETORIC

THE REPUBLIC OF PLATO :
AN ABRIDGED VERSION FOUNDED ON BASIC ENGLISH

HOW TO READ A PAGE

With C. K. Ogden

THE MEANING OF MEANING

Basic

English

PE 1073.5
.R51

and Its Uses

PE1073.5.R51   ST. JOSEPH'S UNIVERSITY   STX

Basic English and its uses,

3 9353 00098 9523

By I. A. RICHARDS
FELLOW OF MAGDALENE COLLEGE, CAMBRIDGE

70674

LONDON
KEGAN PAUL, TRENCH, TRUBNER & CO., LTD.
BROADWAY HOUSE : 68-74 CARTER LANE, E.C.4

First published, 1943

THIS BOOK IS PRODUCED IN COMPLETE
CONFORMITY WITH THE AUTHORIZED
ECONOMY STANDARDS

PRINTED IN GREAT BRITAIN BY
W. & J. MACKAY AND CO., LTD., CHATHAM

THIS is a reconstruction book. It looks to the future and assumes that the reader enjoys a moderate faith in man. It is sustained by the thought that even the immense collective crimes of the present have their encouraging side. In committing them and combating them, men are exhibiting immense virtues—intelligence, courage, steadfastness, initiative—in degrees which should daunt us all. Man's powers to invent, to organize, to dare, and to persist seem indeed almost too much for him. It looks as though, with enough incentive, nothing were too hard. The first mental task of reconstruction is to clear our incentives and choose more positive and permanent goals.

One of these goals is a reasonable degree of communication spread out more evenly over the planet. How to attain that goal is our theme. It is a necessity now ; necessary for human progress, necessary perhaps for human survival. We can no longer risk letting any large section of the human race live in separation, cut off from the fullest possible communication with the rest. When the separated section is powerful, we know what happens. It develops a warped understanding of its own interests, from which must come designs against the interests of the rest of the planet. National aggressions are no accidents, no local freaks of evil inspiration. They are outcomes of spiritual separation. " A man who would live to himself alone must be either a beast or a god," wrote Bacon in echo of Aristotle. That is as true of nations. Being no gods, they become either beasts of prey or their victims. For when the separated nation is weak, technologically undeveloped and helpless, its condition contributes to the same disasters. Such nations tempt others to prey upon them. Prewar China was the great example.

It would be silly, of course, to regard such separation as the only cause of wars ; sillier still to think that differences of language are the only or the chief barriers between nations. Nonetheless, linguistic barriers have their share in the responsibility. No one who knows Central Europe doubts that a common secondary language of discussion—free from partisan charges —would aid immensely in ironing out boundary tensions. No one who knows the Far East doubts that China and Japan must find linguistic access to the thought of the rest of the world if they are to join it in any real fashion. A common medium of communication between peoples rather than between governments is becoming an evident necessity.

The sudden growth of physical communications has sharpened the moral. The plane, after the war, will mix us all up to a degree we have not yet imagined. The radio mixes us up already. And the radio has already been a chief instrument in cultivating those sentiments—of exclusive loyalty to the group, of disloyalty to the planet—which plunge us into wars. It is indeed these technological innovations, or rather their misuse, which we are suffering from. Without canned food, modern metallurgy, and oil, there could be no global war. These new inventions have not been balanced by equal developments in the means of mental transport—and thereby in the spreading of the common truths which would make antagonism and disloyalty harder to cultivate. But these other discoveries are ready to hand—as these pages will attempt to show.

I present first some of the reasons for believing that a simplified form of English is the most practicable common language, and with them, the grounds for doubting whether any artificial language yet devised or imagined could do the same work as adequately. I then describe the form of English which I believe most nearly meets the need, its relationship to unlimited English, and how it has been disengaged from the parent language. I then discuss the teaching of this simplified English and the aid which the sound motion picture, the radio, and other recent inventions can be in this instruction. Finally I show how this simplified form of English—far from offering any threat to full English—may be used to improve and enrich understanding for those of us who are born to the language of Shakespeare and Milton. This last point is indeed of paramount importance. We should be poor servants of the future if in spreading the English language we impaired it. Happily the very constitution of Basic English makes it an influence tending in the other direction. It is no rival to or substitute for an ampler English, where the use of that is feasible. It is an introduction and an exploratory instrument.

I.A.R.

Cambridge, Massachusetts.

Contents

PREFACE   v

I.   ON THE CHOICE OF A SECOND OR WORLD LANGUAGE   9

II.   WHAT BASIC ENGLISH IS   20

III.   THE SIMPLIFICATION OF ENGLISH   40

IV.   AIMS AND POLICIES OF BASIC ENGLISH   62

V.   BASIC ENGLISH TEACHING FILMS   80

VI.   BASIC ENGLISH FOR READING BETTER   91

VII.   IMMEDIATE APPLICATIONS   112

APPENDIX   121

INDEX   125

Chapter One

ON THE CHOICE OF A SECOND OR WORLD LANGUAGE

LET us be clear about some political essentials from the outset. However desirable a common language for all the world may be, as a means of communication between peoples who in their homes speak different tongues, it neither can nor should be imposed by one nation or group of nations upon others. It must come into use freely, as a general convenience, under the urge of the everyday motives of mankind. It must be taken up because men see it to be useful to them—too useful to be neglected. It must serve, and serve immediately, their economic, cultural and social needs. It must give them, right away from the start, a reward in increased possibilities and power. It must spread as the automobile, the electric light, and the telephone or airplane have spread. Only so can it get behind it the drive required to carry through such a gigantic stride toward increased rationality in human affairs.

Secondly, it must be clear from any threat to the economic, moral, cultural, social, or political status or independence of any persons or any people. It must carry no implications of intellectual, technological, or other domination. No one in learning the world language must have excuse for even the least shadow of a feeling that he is submitting to an alien influence or being brought under the power of other groups. Most extensions of communications carry this political threat. To the Siamese of two generations back, with Burma and British Malaya on one side and French Indo-China on the other, the choice between English and French as a school subject brought the question up in a lively fashion. We can guard against this danger only by conceiving a world language in a truly planetary spirit—as a universal medium, not as an extension of the sphere of influence of some one pressure group.

Thirdly, as an obvious corollary, no one should be encouraged, far less compelled, to give up the language which is natively his, and adopt another. That usually entails too high a price in personal and cultural values to be tolerable. The common secondary language must be such that it can be learned without any sacrifice of men's ability in their own primary languages.

A*

It can, in fact, be so easy to learn that much time now given ineffectually to foreign languages would be freed for further study and improvement in primary languages—than which nothing is more important.

Fourthly, and more positively, the learning and use of the common language should be symbolic of the learner's participation in the common human political effort, a sign that he recognizes the claim upon him of the world community—beyond that of his regional, racial, or cultural group. Only so will the spread of a world language be linked with the greatest of the unused sources of power—man's new need, corresponding to his new knowledge, for a loyalty larger than any he has yet known. As the use of Latin in the Middle Ages fed, and in turn was supported by, the dream of the Holy Roman Empire, as the Chinese script once embodied the spirit of the Middle Kingdom, so the world language of our age, if it is to fit the larger world we live in, must be the instrument of purposes transcending those of any nation or group of present nations. It must be identified with a world view which values nations only as they contribute to a world aim.

For this reason it would be better not to talk of it as an *international* language. Jeremy Bentham, who coined that word, would to-day be the first to insist that the purposes and practices of nations (those typical Benthamic fictions) in their dealings with one another are man's chief disgrace. International affairs are a sad and ghastly record of greed and fear and fraud and fury. These are the necessary faults of the nation as an institution, and while there is one nation still existing there must be others. Their very being derives from mutual restraint, and " foreign relations " are the outcome. World affairs should be carefully distinguished, though they must at present, of course, grow out of the happier impulses of nations. *Supranational* would be the better fitted word. The common language must carry and be carried by the supranational impulse, and be the organ of the supranational mind.

Free adoption, absence of all threats of domination of any type, protection for primary languages, symbolization of supranational aims—these are some of the necessary political conditions for the coming into currency of a world secondary language. They have to be reconciled with equally necessary psychological and linguistic conditions. Let us consider these. The political considerations we have outlined seem to argue against any existing national language as a candidate. The other considerations weigh more heavily still against any artificial, constructed language. We shall take the psychological problems first.

Dreams of a universal language that would bring the nations to better understanding have, of course, for centuries haunted the imaginations of the generous-minded. Laments for the decay of Latin, proposals for renovating and reviving it, enthusiasms for Esperanto, Ido, Novial, Nulango—with these we are familiar. The trouble is that these generous designs are too rarely balanced by a concrete, living sense of actualities and practicalities. " Crackpot schemes ! " is the current description of them in the mouths of hardheaded persons. This is a serious matter, since it is to hardheaded, practical men that we must look for effective action. We shall do well to examine the grounds for this adverse opinion as to artificial languages before considering the proposals to use some form of an existing language.

The root criticism of any revived or artificial language, however well designed, is that the immediate incentive which would make enough people learn and use one is lacking. We all want a better world. We may all agree that a world auxiliary language would help. The cynical opinion, which dissents and says that the less we understand one another the better, will not be considered here. We may all wish that everyone would learn such a language. But these wishes, however strong they might be, will never be strong enough to make enough people put enough time into learning an artificial language as a speculative investment. If you are to go to the trouble of learning a language you need to feel that you will get a return for your toil this very year. A man may plant an orchard and wait six years for his apples ; but six months is long enough to wait for verbs and prepositions to bear fruit. You do not want access merely to a limited and artificial literature, or to a few other speakers and correspondents. You want a vast and undelayed expansion of your contacts. The feeling that you are contributing in your small way to an idealistic but doubtful future is an inadequate motive. It is sad, but it is so. The realization that the speakers of any artificial language are unlikely to increase as rapidly as the inhabitants, say, of Madagascar is a fatal damper.

Of course, if by world decree or world agreement all children everywhere were to be taught, say, Novial, and if most things worth reading or listening to were to be made available in that language, the prospect would be different. But here again we must separate dreams from actualities. Who is seriously expecting anything of that sort in any foreseeable future? And on what sort of political judgment would such an expectation be based? Any of the many new artificial languages now in competition with one another or in preparation would need decades of widespread use before any recommendation for universal adoption would be conceivable.

Linguistic considerations confirm these doubts as to the feasibility of artificial languages. Languages are shaped by use rather than by design. They acquire their powers—their suppleness, their overtones, their resourcefulness, their ability to serve human needs, their almost divine capacity to make a speaker wiser than he knows (and their devilish capacity to make a fool of him)—from use. Willy-nilly, the situations in which we use words and hear them used control them. Long-established languages have been hammered and wrought, broken and remade, at every point, in countless ways which only the biggest and best of dictionaries can show in detail. The amazing interdependence of our words comes to them from use. Their forms and their meanings are survivors of a terrific elimination contest. No artificial language can acquire a tithe of such richness of interdependence, however cunningly the resources of roots are exploited, without centuries of wide and varied use. Until this mutuality between its words is gained, literature in the serious sense is all but impossible. So is wit, so is real depth of emotional communication. A new auxiliary language would have to be used through many lifetimes before it could offer a learner possibilities of general communication equal to those given through even an inferior handling of any of the major languages, which have been through this process and been fitted by use to human affairs. The speaker of Esperanto who doubts this is probably importing into the interactions of its meanings many nuances from his mother tongue, nuances which will be inoperative for persons with a different background. With a simplified form of a living language these discrepancies are reduced. Its meanings are held in place by the extent of the common use its words have been put to.

This limitation will be felt least in writing or speech with a scientific content, where many words stand for rigidly defined ideas and are relatively invariable in meaning from one sentence to another. This is the writing or speech that is easiest to translate. But in most use of language no such rigidity holds. In the discussion of affairs, the exchange of opinion, the pursuit of common human purposes, the adjustment of variant views ; in most uses of speech except the plain statement of well-explored and agreed facts ; in nearly everything but greetings, bromides, phatic communion, and the more humdrum parts of trade and the sciences, matters are very different. In all this, in all the employments for which a general world language is most needed, words accommodate their meanings to the other words that accompany them, in myriad ways easier to analyse than to predict. But it is through these very shifts that our languages serve us ; their words are controlled in these shifts by the collective experimentation that has gone to their shaping. No designer of a new language can supply out of his linguistic acumen (no matter how great it is) a substitute for this process. To compare organs of comparable delicacy and complexity, no physiologist could design a digestive system able to adjust itself to meet all challenges from the cook ! Our languages, like our digestive tracts, are products of experimentation beyond the scope of any inventor.

Such are, in brief, the chief arguments against auxiliary languages of the Esperanto type. They point to this. If there is to be a common language it must be a simplified, but not denatured, form of one of the world's existing major languages. That would give the learner immediate access to innumerable speakers. It would lead into the parent language and so give the learner—up to the limits of his capacities—admission to a vast literature. Being part of the major language it would take from it the resourcefulness and interdependence, the hard-won mutual adjustment of its parts, needed if it is to serve the general purposes of mankind. Thus, two of our three requirements would be met ; the objections to Esperanto-type languages would be avoided. But what of the third, the political problem ? Is it conceivable that the very natural objections of individuals and nations to having the language of one section of the earth's population put into such a privileged position can be overcome ? Will not the cry, " This is linguistic and cultural imperialism ! " be as fatal as the charge of being a " crackpot scheme " ?

It is worth noting, first, that this cry is not in fact raised by those who would have to learn English, for example, but by supporters of one or other of the artificial languages. Neither those who learn English nor those who teach it as a foreign language have in general any feeling that they are submitting to or furthering a process of intellectual subjugation. On the contrary, they are more likely to feel that they are helping themselves or others to resist such influences. The Chinese, for example, are not in the least afraid of English. What they do often feel is that an excessive amount of time given up to learning English may be damaging to the study of their own language. And that, they rightly believe, would be disastrous. In general, the notion that the spread of a language is a step toward political control is not borne out by recent history. The history of the nationalist movement in India is an instructive instance. Its leaders and its chief supporters are speakers of English and sometimes use it rather as their first than as their second language.

Such arguments, however, take their force rather from feelings than from facts. And here the conduct of the English-speaking powers after the victory will be a decisive factor. In comparison with the attitudes they display in the peace conferences and in the reconstruction programme, most other considerations will seem but academic. Whatever comes from imperialist sources will rightly be thought to smell of imperialism. The world will watch whether the majority feeling against all forms of domination, which is so immensely strong both in the United States and in the British Commonwealth, is translated into action—whether, in brief, these countries are able to live up to their political consciences. It will note, too, we may hope, that police duties are one thing, exploitation another. In any case, upon the behaviour of these powers the prospects of English as the common second language will largely depend. If their acts seem animated by a universal enough spirit, these prospects are likely to be bright indeed.

The world's need for a common language will quite certainly be augmented beyond measure in the very near future. The airplanes of tomorrow will see to that. So will the resultant needs for world-wide controls of all kinds—sanitary, economic, commercial—and for the supply and distribution of information and news. We are only at the beginning of the reporting age. All this will call for (is already calling for) an immediately available common language. And the most immediately available language is English. Furthermore, English is in many ways the language best suited to the task. It is not merely prevalent, but it is prevalent for good reasons.

English speakers are parties to the case and should find it hard to form an impartial judgment. But let us try for a few pages to see what a neutral judge would have to consider. If he is to keep the general interests of the planet in view, he will have to ask at least the following questions :

1. Which of the existing major languages can be made easiest for learners in general ?

2. Which at present contains the most universally useful literature in the widest sense ?

3. Which is already used—fully or in some considerable degree —by the most people ?

4. Which has already been learned on the largest scale by those with other native tongues, and taught as a foreign language most extensively in educational systems ?

5. Which, by reason of its history and the uses which have been made of it in the past, is most likely to serve best as a bridge between peoples who will and should continue to use their own languages as before ?

6. Which lends itself most readily to the new means of instruction—by film, radio, and recordings—that are being developed and seem likely to take some of the burden off the teacher's back in the near future ?

1. Spanish, as the major language with the most phonetic spelling, makes a claim here. But phonetic clarity of spelling is only one factor—not the most important—in estimating ease of learning. Far more important is the *amount* of the language— in vocabulary and in grammar—that has to be mastered before the student is able to go on in the language as we all go on in our own languages, without grammar books or bilingual dictionaries, just by taking in more of it with the aid of what we have already. The two languages which lead in this respect are English and, much more doubtfully, Chinese. We shall see in Chapter Two why and how English is able to cover a vast range of needs with a very small vocabulary and a very simple set of constructions. Three times as much Spanish, it is estimated, would be needed to cover comparable ground. Therefore a learner of Spanish, in comparison with a learner of English, properly taught, takes three times as long at least to reach the stage above described. This is due to the structures of the two languages. If this situation were reversed and Spanish were as much easier than English as it is harder in this respect, there might be little doubt that Spanish should be the world's " second

language." But unfortunately Spanish is not easier. The Spanish verb system gets in the way. The conjugation of the verb by inflection, that is by modification of or addition to the root or stem, does, it is true, make personal pronouns as subjects unnecessary except in an occasional ambiguous situation. Yet this economy of pronouns is far outweighed by the increased learning load of the verb changes themselves. Simplify them as much as possible, to the utmost degree compatible with keeping the language still Spanish, and they yet remain a formidable obstacle. Nor can German, French, Italian, or Russian promise the learner easier progress than Spanish.

A further point may be touched on here. A simplified " beginner's " form may offer something of a threat to the parent language in some cases. A Spanish- or Russian-made-easy, if it is made really easy, must use non-Spanish and non-Russian forms which could in time considerably alter the forms— typically the verb inflections—needed for clarity. They could act as a corrupting agency, especially for populations that have not yet advanced very far into a secure mastery of these languages. In South America and in Asiatic Russia there are large masses of population that are thus exposed. The simplification (whether introduced by design or through the " accidental " pressures of use) that would attend the attempts to use these languages all over the planet might, therefore, be damaging to them as finely developed instruments of communication.

The case with a language that uses word order rather than inflections as its chief grammatical device is very different. A simplified essential vocabulary and the avoidance of specially difficult constructions offer there no such threat to the integrity of the rest of the language. The constructions the simplified language uses are a selection only of the normal forms of the parent language ; they leave the forms that are not used unaffected. In brief, there is nothing to unlearn in passing from simple English to the full use of the language. There is no deviation and therefore no danger. Simplified modes of English— those used by relatively unlettered learners—serve and have served for centuries as fenders against the shocks and strains any language undergoes under rapid diffusion. Basic English might be described as that part of English that can suffer least at the hands (tongues, rather) of new adult learners. We shall see later that this factor has entered historically into the development of its forms through the centuries.

2. The second question, " Which language has the most universally useful literature ? " is less capable of a factual answer. Value judgments come in. But the range of technical and scientific writings in English is undoubtedly as wide as those in German (the closest competitor). Its poetry is far greater, in world opinion. Its literature of discussion—especially its political literature—is unrivalled. Further, it has proved able, since the days of the King James Bible, to take in other literature by translation with peculiar felicity. There seems to be no question that English wins on this count.

3. Into the third question, estimates of populations enter. Population figures for the future must be largely guesswork. With a world revolution of such depth in progress, anything may happen to recent trends. The British nations and the United States have been losing ground. Russia and some of the South American states seem to be due for explosive leaps as industrialization, for example, takes effect. But no one yet knows what the fundamental factors are. They may be economic, but they may equally well be psychologic. Furthermore, few accurate figures for the native speakers of any language are available. Published estimates differ immensely. Questions as to mutual intelligibility between dialects come in. The degree of mastery of a language which makes a student a member of a speech community is indeterminate. . . However, for what they are worth and subject to every sort of reserve, the following guesses in millions may indicate something like the present position :

English 200, North Chinese 200, Russian 120, German 100, Spanish 100, French 75, Japanese 80, Cantonese 60, Bengali 60, Italian 50, Portuguese 50.

4. Estimates of those who have acquired these languages are subject to still more doubt. Exact figures are unobtainable. But in view of the programmes, if not of the actualities, of the world's chief educational systems, it is safe to say that opportunity to learn English has been offered to more students in the last century than has been the case with any other " foreign language."

5. As to which would serve as the most effective bridge between peoples, three factors have favoured English. One is the geographical spread of the language. It has been in wider use in more different parts of the earth than any other living language. It has been an administrative language in every continent. It has been the trade language of the Pacific, and a main vehicle of the spread of commercial and financial practice for two cen-

turies. And it has carried sports, fashions, and modern techniques more variously and more widely than any other language. Recently the English-speaking motion picture has taken a hand in the process. Conversely, the limited spread of Spanish in India, China, the U.S.S.R., and Europe is a strong argument against the world future of that language.

The second factor is the peculiar mixture of Germanic and Latin roots which is characteristic of English. The manipulative structural essentials of the language are largely Germanic ; the important " content words " are very evenly divided between the two sources. This makes it a singularly effective bridge between two great groups of speakers.

The third factor is the " melting-pot " function of the United States and the Dominions. There for a century, English-speaking communities have been assimilating non-English immigrants on an enormous scale. (South America has done likewise, in both Spanish and Portuguese, but on a minor scale.) This process has maintained those characteristics of English which make a limited acquaintance with it go the furthest way. It has kept it a language suited to the needs of those who do not learn much of it, who learn it not as scholars—" for ornament and reputation "—but " to the benefit and use of men."

6. With the application of motion pictures and radio to language teaching we shall be concerned in a later chapter. That such modes of teaching have a vast future is certain. It will there be argued that a simplified English possesses certain characteristics which fit it uniquely to these modes. The learning of any language can be greatly aided by properly constructed sound films, but the learning of English, it seems reasonable to believe, can be eased and speeded to a far higher degree. The reasons for so thinking will become clear after an account has been given of the structure of the simplest necessary English, and its reliance on verbs of motion and on visual modes of explanation.

Answers to these six questions, then, converge. They point to one conclusion : a priority for English as the world's " second language " in the interests of everyone. To speakers of other tongues this will no doubt seem a very natural conclusion for any English-speaking author to arrive at. Probably the assertion that it will be for others' advantage even more than for our own will seem hardly sincere. " Native speakers of English are bad linguists and lazy," it may be said. " Therefore let everyone else learn English while they give their attention to getting the better of other peoples in further ways." And to such accusations it is hard for us to reply. Our alleged incompetence as linguists is at least doubtful. On the other point, this may perhaps be said. A general adoption of English as a second language might well put the English-speaking peoples at a certain disadvantage ; others would use two languages ; most of us would probably acquire only English. But that sort of argument would at best occasion grins abroad. At home it should prompt us to keep up foreign languages ourselves and work toward improvements in the techniques of learning them comparable in some measure to the improvements in the learning of English that are now possible.

Chapter Two

WHAT BASIC ENGLISH IS

RUDOLPH HESS, shortly before his flight to England, announced at a party conference that when the Nazis had won, English would become " a minor Germanic dialect of no world importance." We have glanced at some of the linguistic reasons why that would have been regrettable. His utterance contrasts well with Bismarck's view that the most significant event of the nineteenth century was the acceptance of English as the language of North America. We have now to see why English can be made easier for any learner than any other major language, how a streamlined English suited to the general affairs of the world has been produced, and what has been and may be done with this form of English.

Basic English is English made simple by limiting the number of its words to 850, and by cutting down the rules for using them to the smallest number necessary for the clear statement of ideas. And this is done without change in the normal order and behaviour of these words in everyday English. This is the first point to make clear. Basic English, though it has only 850 words, is still normal English. It is limited in its words and its rules, but it keeps to the regular forms of English. And though it is designed to give the learner as little trouble as possible, it is no more strange to the eyes of my readers than these lines, which are in fact in Basic English. The reader to whom all this is new may get some amusement from attempting to see for himself, before I give a fuller account of the system, where I first went into Basic on this page.

The second point to make clear is that even with so small a word list and so simple a structure it is possible to say in Basic English anything needed for the general purposes of everyday existence—in business, trade, industry, science, medical work— in all the arts of living, in all the exchanges of knowledge, desires, beliefs, opinions, and news which are the chief work of a language. It is true that if we go outside the field of general interests and into special branches of the sciences, the arts or the trades, we will have to have other words, not listed among the 850. But the senses of these other words may be made clear in footnotes with the 850 ; or by teaching given through Basic English.

Or they may be seen in the *General Basic English Dictionary*, which, using only the Basic words, gives the senses of twenty thousand other English words. In this way Basic becomes a framework in which words needed for special purposes take their place and from and through which they take their senses. A knowledge of the 850 and of the rules by which they are put together is enough, however, for talk and writing on all everyday general levels.

It would not be hard to put all this book has to say into Basic. It would be clear but not very bright reading. The same words —because there are only 850 of them—would keep coming back again and again. A reader who has the rest of the English language gets a little tired of Basic writing after a time. So I return (with this word *return*, which is not one of the Basic words) to a less confined medium. I have shown, I hope, in the last two paragraphs that Basic is normal English when properly written, and that it can say somewhat complicated things in a reasonably lucid and acceptable fashion.

But this last point no longer needs demonstration. Far too much has been written in Basic on too many subjects (*see* Appendix) for doubt to linger, in the minds of any who have studied the literature, as to the scope and powers of this miniature English. Of course, there is bad Basic and good Basic—as there is bad English and good English. The fact that many people write English wretchedly is no evidence that English is a poor language. Basic, thanks to the care with which its specification was prepared, has been able to adopt as its ruling principle from the outset, " If it is bad English, it is bad Basic."

The third most important point about Basic is that it is not merely a list of words, governed by a minimum apparatus of essential English grammar, but a highly organized system designed throughout to be as easy as possible for a learner who is totally ignorant of English *or of any related language*. It is a language for all the world, not just for those who happen to have some related language as their mother tongue. It is easier for them, naturally enough. The ideas its words carry accord more readily with theirs, its constructions parallel theirs more closely. And, no doubt, by exploiting those parallels, it might have been possible to give them, in some slight degree, a privileged entrance to English. But that would have been at the cost of a radical injustice to speakers of languages remote from English. On the most neutral grounds, the Chinese have a very strong claim to consideration by framers of a world language. There are so many of them, and the part they should play in the world should be second to none. A simplified English, if put forward as a planetary language, must be made as accessible as possible to peoples other than those of Indo-European tongues—and it so happens, through the unique peculiarities of English, that this could be done without any measurable cost in added difficulty for cognate language groups. This third point about Basic is, then, that it is a simplification of English designed equally, so far as the structure of English permits, for users of all languages whatsoever.

The fourth main point is this. If a language is to be easy to learn we must not only cut its words down to a minimum and regularize its grammar ; we must also study very carefully the meanings of every one of its words and decide upon the central, pivotal or key meaning of each one of them. Parallel to the reduction and ordering of its vocabulary, there must be a reduction and ordering of the meanings of the words it recommends. It should be obvious that the task of mastering a set of words will be immensely lightened if, for each one of them, the central meaning be presented first. This central meaning will be the meaning by reference to which its other meanings can be most easily understood. All this has been done with Basic, and yet of the many distinctive characteristics of Basic, this so far has received least attention. It may seem a refined point, but it is essential. Clarity upon it makes all the difference in the world to our conception of language learning. A set of meanings which, if presented in one order, is merely a burden upon the memory can become, if offered in another order, a pleasurable exercise of intelligence. Many examples will appear in what follows. Here I need only say that this selective ordering of the meanings of the Basic words was quite half the task which its originator, Mr. C. K. Ogden, undertook and carried through (*see* pp. 52-54 and 56).

Here let me sketch the story of the discovery of Basic English. I say " discovery " rather than " invention," to stress the point that Basic English was a possibility inherent in the development of English, something needing to be disengaged from full English, not something made up. It had its origin, perhaps, in 1920 when Ogden and I were considering the analysis and control of the meanings of the word " meaning " and writing a book we called *The Meaning of Meaning*. But in a sense Basic English dates back earlier, for Ogden was already deeply read in the history of attempts to frame a universal language and much concerned with the problem. He was then collecting materials on " word magic " for a major work on the influence of language on thought.

In our joint work we came to the theory and practice of definition. In comparing definitions—definitions of anything, from a sense quality to a force and from a rabbit to a concept—we were struck by the fact that whatever you are defining, certain words keep coming back into your definitions. Define them, and with them you could define anything. That suggests that there might be some limited set of words in terms of which the meanings of all other words might be stated. If so, then a very limited language—limited in its vocabulary but comprehensive in its scope—would be possible. This was by no means a new idea ; it has haunted many analytic philosophers through the centuries, among whom Leibnitz and Bishop Wilkins are the best known ; but it set Ogden on the track which later led to Basic English.

This initial idea had many discouraging aspects. Ogden has an abnormally developed capacity for verbal experimentation—a natural gift for rephrasing which he has systematically cultivated. Perhaps he is the first man to take a talent possessed by many of the best scholar-journalists and develop it deliberately into an instrument of experimental linguistic research. A little of this experimentation soon made two things dauntingly evident: that even if such a limited language could perhaps be worked out in some ten years, it would be too abstract and difficult for practical use. Furthermore, as it seemed then, in 1920, such a language would not be in the least like everyday English. It would be an academic curiosity, not a general instrument for the common purposes of the world.

Ogden found the way out of these difficulties in part through study of the nature of the verb—aided by some suggestive hints from Jeremy Bentham, whose writings on language he was to edit. But chiefly it was due to his extraordinarily persistent experimentation. Saying the same thing in other ways became more than a game for him ; it became a passion—pursuing constantly a clear-cut goal, a minimum comprehensive English, streamlined at every point to offer the least possible resistance to a learner and yet render him at the earliest moment the maximum amount of service. Though Ogden was blessed with exceptionally able collaborators—among whom Miss L. W. Lockhart and the late Dr. F. G. Crookshank must be mentioned

—Basic English is essentially the creation of a heightened gift of critical experimentation in a mind unusually well fortified by the relevant linguistic sciences and disciplines.

By 1927 it was clear that an English able to cover the necessary ground and limited to less than a thousand words was feasible. What remained was chiefly a statesman's problem : how best to reconcile all the rival claims—simplicity, economy, regularity, ease of learning, scope, clarity, naturalness, grace ; how to balance this local advantage against that for the common good. These were points which could only be worked out through prolonged and very tedious trial and comparison. It is worth remarking that the final design for Basic English was fully tested as against possible alternative designs during this final period and before the first publications in 1929.

So much, for the present, as to how Basic came into being. That such a small number of words is able to take over the work—at certain levels and for certain purposes—of the rest of the language is a very surprising fact. In later pages I will be attempting to say how they do it. But first we have to be clear about the sorts of words there are in Basic. Only then will we see how they may be put together to do the work of other words.

The last *paragraph* was again in Basic. If I now *translate* (put) some of it back into fuller, English, *italicizing* (putting in sloping print) the words that are not in Basic, that may *suggest* something (give some idea) of the process :

So much, for the *moment*, as to how Basic *originated*. That so *few* words *can deputize*—at certain levels and for certain purposes—for the *remainder* of the language is *astonishing*. In a later *chapter* I shall *try* to *explain* how they do it. But first we have to be clear about the sorts of words there are in Basic. Only then will we see how they may be *combined* to *convey* the meanings of other words.

On pages 26-27 will be seen the Basic Word List. Its 850 words are divided into three main classes. There are six hundred names of things, one hundred and fifty names of qualities (adjectives) and one hundred " operations," as Ogden calls them : words that put the others into significant relationship with one another. It is these one hundred operations or structure words which most need our attention here. Indeed they are in many ways the most important words in Basic. They are those that give the learner and the teacher of Basic the greater part of their trouble ; they are those upon which the simplicity of Basic chiefly depends ; they are those whose study gives most insight into the structure not only of Basic but of full English as well ; and they are those from which we can learn most about the nature, the resources, and the limitations of language in general. A careful study of these one hundred words is a course in grammar, in linguistics, and in theory of meaning.[1] Here, however, we are concerned only with how the right choice of these one hundred words completely changes the prospects for English as a world language.

A glance down the operations column, the first column of the Basic Word List (pp. 26-27), shows that the first eighteen words (from *come* to *will*) are what are usually called verbs. Ogden, for sound but not altogether simple reasons, prefers to call them " operators." The work they are capable of doing is unlike that of other English verbs in certain important respects which will be noted later. They may be divided into four sets. The first ten (*come* to *take*) are names of irreducibly simple acts. *Seem* somewhat resists this classification or indeed any description. It is easiest to think of it as complementary to *be*. (We *seem* wise and good perhaps ; we *are* perhaps foolish and bad.) But the others name what we do, or what things do, and between them they cover our doings, and the doings of things, in a peculiarly comprehensive fashion. Into the meanings of other verbs comes some component able to be carried by one or more of these operators (as *enter*, for example, has the meaning of *come in*, and *meditate* has a meaning which may be carried by *give thought* or *take thought*). And this is what has been meant by the claim that Basic has " no verbs." Its use of these superverbs or operators allows it to dispense with the rest.

Next come *be*, *do*, and *have* which do such a lion's share of the work in English either as full verbs or as auxiliaries. Then come *say*, *see*, *send*. These are luxury conveniences in Basic and not strictly indispensable. We could cover their uses with other Basic words. When we *say* something, we *put* it into words ; when we *see* something it *is* in view or we *have* it before our eyes ; when we *send* someone we *make* him *go*, and so on. But these periphrases would be awkward, and these three words are

---

[1]Such a course prepared for classroom use may be found in *Words at Work* by Miss Christine Gibson of the Harvard Commission on English Language Studies.

BASIC ENGLISH WORD LIST

OPERATIONS 100

COME, GET, GIVE, GO, KEEP, LET, MAKE, PUT, SEEM, TAKE, BE, DO, HAVE, SAY, SEE, SEND, MAY, WILL, ABOUT, ACROSS, AFTER, AGAINST, AMONG, AT, BEFORE, BETWEEN, BY, DOWN, FROM, IN, OFF, ON, OVER, THROUGH, TO, UNDER, UP, WITH, AS, FOR, OF, TILL, THAN, A, THE, ALL, ANY

THINGS

400 General

ACCOUNT	EDUCATION	METAL	SENSE
ACT	EFFECT	MIDDLE	SERVANT
ADDITION	END	MILK	SEX
ADJUSTMENT	ERROR	MIND	SHADE
ADVERTISEMENT	EVENT	MINE	SHAKE
AGREEMENT	EXAMPLE	MINUTE	SHAME
AIR	EXCHANGE	MIST	SHOCK
AMOUNT	EXISTENCE	MONEY	SIDE
AMUSEMENT	EXPANSION	MONTH	SIGN
ANIMAL	EXPERIENCE	MORNING	SILK
ANSWER	EXPERT	MOTHER	SILVER
APPARATUS	FACT	MOTION	SISTER
APPROVAL	FALL	MOUNTAIN	SIZE
ARGUMENT	FAMILY	MOVE	SKY
ART	FATHER	MUSIC	SLEEP
ATTACK	FEAR	NAME	SLIP
ATTEMPT	FEELING	NATION	SLOPE
ATTENTION	FICTION	NEED	SMASH
ATTRACTION	FIELD	NEWS	SMELL
AUTHORITY	FIGHT	NIGHT	SMILE
BACK	FIRE	NOISE	SMOKE
BALANCE	FLAME	NOTE	SNEEZE
BASE	FLIGHT	NUMBER	SNOW
BEHAVIOR	FLOWER	OBSERVATION	SOAP
BELIEF	FOLD	OFFER	SOCIETY
BIRTH	FOOD	OIL	SON
BIT	FORCE	OPERATION	SONG
BITE	FORM	OPINION	SORT
BLOOD	FRIEND	ORDER	SOUND
BLOW	FRONT	ORGANIZATION	SOUP
BODY	FRUIT	ORNAMENT	SPACE
BRASS	GLASS	OWNER	STAGE
BREAD	GOLD	PAGE	START
BREATH	GOVERNMENT	PAIN	STATEMENT
BROTHER	GRAIN	PAINT	STEAM
BUILDING	GRASS	PAPER	STEEL
BURN	GRIP	PART	STEP
BURST	GROUP	PASTE	STITCH
BUSINESS	GROWTH	PAYMENT	STONE
BUTTER	GUIDE	PEACE	STOP
CANVAS	HARBOR	PERSON	STORY
CARE	HARMONY	PLACE	STRETCH
CAUSE	HATE	PLANT	STRUCTURE
CHALK	HEARING	PLAY	SUBSTANCE
CHANCE	HEAT	PLEASURE	SUGAR
CHANGE	HELP	POINT	SUGGESTION
CLOTH	HISTORY	POISON	SUMMER

200 Picturable

ANGLE	KNEE
ANT	KNIFE
APPLE	KNOT
ARCH	LEAF
ARM	LEG
ARMY	LIBRARY
BABY	LINE
BAG	LIP
BALL	LOCK
BAND	MAP
BASIN	MATCH
BASKET	MONKEY
BATH	MOON
BED	MOUTH
BEE	MUSCLE
BELL	NAIL
BERRY	NECK
BIRD	NEEDLE
BLADE	NERVE
BOARD	NET
BOAT	NOSE
BONE	NUT
BOOK	OFFICE
BOOT	ORANGE
BOTTLE	OVEN
BOX	PARCEL
BOY	PEN
BRAIN	PENCIL
BRAKE	PICTURE
BRANCH	PIG
BRICK	PIN
BRIDGE	PIPE
BRUSH	PLANE
BUCKET	PLATE
BULB	PLOUGH
BUTTON	POCKET
CAKE	POT
CAMERA	POTATO
CARD	PRISON
CART	PUMP
CARRIAGE	RAIL
CAT	RAT
CHAIN	RECEIPT
CHEESE	RING
CHEST	ROD
CHIN	ROOF
CHURCH	ROOT

QUALITIES

100 General

ABLE, ACID, ANGRY, AUTOMATIC, BEAUTIFUL, BLACK, BOILING, BRIGHT, BROKEN, BROWN, CHEAP, CHEMICAL, CHIEF, CLEAN, CLEAR, COMMON, COMPLEX, CONSCIOUS, CUT, DEEP, DEPENDENT, EARLY, ELASTIC, ELECTRIC, EQUAL, FAT, FERTILE, FIRST, FIXED, FLAT, FREE, FREQUENT, FULL, GENERAL, GOOD, GREAT, GREY, HANGING, HAPPY, HARD, HEALTHY, HIGH, HOLLOW, IMPORTANT, KIND, LIKE, YOUNG

50 Opposites

AWAKE, BAD, BENT, BITTER, BLUE, CERTAIN, COLD, COMPLETE, CRUEL, DARK, DEAD, DEAR, DELICATE, DIFFERENT, DIRTY, DRY, FALSE, FEEBLE, FEMALE, FOOLISH, FUTURE, GREEN, ILL, LAST, LATE, LEFT, LOOSE, LOUD, LOW, MIXED, NARROW, OLD, OPPOSITE, PUBLIC, ROUGH, SAD, SAFE, SECRET, SHORT, SHUT, SIMPLE, SLOW, SMALL, SOFT, SOLID, SPECIAL, STRANGE

NO	COLOR	HOPE	PORTER	SURPRISE	CLOCK	SCHOOL	MALE	WHITE
OTHER	COMFORT	HOUR	POSITION	SWIM	CLOUD	SCISSORS	MARRIED	WRONG
SOME	COMMITTEE	HUMOR	POWDER	SYSTEM	COAT	SCREW	MATERIAL	
SUCH	COMPANY	ICE	POWER	TALK	COLLAR	SEED	MEDICAL	SUMMARY
THAT	COMPARISON	IDEA	PRICE	TASTE	COMB	SHEEP	MILITARY	OF
THIS	COMPETITION	IMPULSE	PRINT	TAX	CORD	SHELF	NATURAL	RULES
I	CONDITION	INCREASE	PROCESS	TEACHING	COW	SHIP	NECESSARY	
HE	CONNECTION	INDUSTRY	PRODUCE	TENDENCY	CUP	SHIRT	NEW	PLURALS IN 'S.'
YOU	CONTROL	INK	PROFIT	TEST	CURTAIN	SHOE	NORMAL	
WHO	COOK	INSECT	PROPERTY	THEORY	CUSHION	SKIN	OPEN	DERIVATIVES IN 'ER,' 'ING,' 'ED' FROM 300 NOUNS.
AND	COPPER	INSTRUMENT	PROSE	THING	DOG	SKIRT	PARALLEL	
BECAUSE	COPY	INSURANCE	PROTEST	THOUGHT	DOOR	SNAKE	PAST	
BUT	CORK	INTEREST	PULL	THUNDER	DRAIN	SOCK	PHYSICAL	
OR	COTTON	INVENTION	PUNISHMENT	TIME	DRAWER	SPADE	POLITICAL	ADVERBS IN 'LY' FROM QUALIFIERS.
IF	COUGH	IRON	PURPOSE	TIN	DRESS	SPONGE	POOR	
THOUGH	COUNTRY	JELLY	PUSH	TOP	DROP	SPOON	POSSIBLE	
WHILE	COVER	JOIN	QUALITY	TOUCH	EAR	SPRING	PRESENT	DEGREE WITH 'MORE' AND 'MOST.'
HOW	CRACK	JOURNEY	QUESTION	TRADE	EGG	SQUARE	PRIVATE	
WHEN	CREDIT	JUDGE	RAIN	TRANSPORT	ENGINE	STAMP	PROBABLE	
WHERE	CRIME	JUMP	RANGE	TRICK	EYE	STAR	QUICK	QUESTIONS BY INVERSION AND 'DO.'
WHY	CRUSH	KICK	RATE	TROUBLE	FACE	STATION	QUIET	
AGAIN	CRY	KISS	RAY	TURN	FARM	STEM	READY	
EVER	CURRENT	KNOWLEDGE	REACTION	TWIST	FEATHER	STICK	RED	OPERATORS AND PRONOUNS CONJUGATE IN FULL.
FAR	CURVE	LAND	READING	UNIT	FINGER	STOCKING	REGULAR	
FORWARD	DAMAGE	LANGUAGE	REASON	USE	FISH	STOMACH	RESPONSIBLE	
HERE	DANGER	LAUGH	RECORD	VALUE	FLAG	STORE	RIGHT	
NEAR	DAUGHTER	LAW	REGRET	VERSE	FLOOR	STREET	ROUND	MEASUREMENT, NUMERALS, CURRENCY, CALENDAR, AND INTERNATIONAL TERMS IN ENGLISH FORM.
NOW	DAY	LEAD	RELATION	VESSEL	FLY	SUN	SAME	
OUT	DEATH	LEARNING	RELIGION	VIEW	FOOT	TABLE	SECOND	
STILL	DEBT	LEATHER	REPRESENTATIVE	VOICE	FORK	TAIL	SEPARATE	
THEN	DECISION	LETTER	REQUEST	WALK	FOWL	THREAD	SERIOUS	
THERE	DEGREE	LEVEL	RESPECT	WAR	FRAME	THROAT	SHARP	
TOGETHER	DESIGN	LIFT	REST	WASH	GARDEN	THUMB	SMOOTH	
WELL	DESIRE	LIGHT	REWARD	WASTE	GIRL	TICKET	STICKY	
ALMOST	DESTRUCTION	LIMIT	RHYTHM	WATER	GLOVE	TOE	STIFF	
ENOUGH	DETAIL	LINEN	RICE	WAVE	GOAT	TONGUE	STRAIGHT	
EVEN	DEVELOPMENT	LIQUID	RIVER	WAX	GUN	TOOTH	STRONG	
LITTLE	DIGESTION	LIST	ROAD	WAY	HAIR	TOWN	SUDDEN	
MUCH	DIRECTION	LOOK	ROLL	WEATHER	HAMMER	TRAIN	SWEET	
NOT	DISCOVERY	LOSS	ROOM	WEEK	HAND	TRAY	TALL	
ONLY	DISCUSSION	LOVE	RUB	WEIGHT	HAT	TREE	THICK	
QUITE	DISEASE	MACHINE	RULE	WIND	HEAD	TROUSERS	TIGHT	
SO	DISGUST	MAN	RUN	WINE	HEART	UMBRELLA	TIRED	
VERY	DISTANCE	MANAGER	SALT	WINTER	HORN	WALL	TRUE	
TOMORROW	DISTRIBUTION	MARK	SAND	WOMAN	HORSE	WATCH	VIOLENT	
YESTERDAY	DIVISION	MARKET	SCALE	WOOD	HOSPITAL	WHEEL	WAITING	
NORTH	DOUBT	MASS	SCIENCE	WOOL	HOUSE	WHIP	WARM	
SOUTH	DRINK	MEAL	SEA	WORD	ISLAND	WHISTLE	WET	
EAST	DRIVING	MEASURE	SEAT	WORK	JEWEL.	WINDOW	WIDE	
WEST	DUST	MEAT	SECRETARY	WOUND	KETTLE	WING	WISE	
PLEASE	EARTH	MEETING	SELECTION	WRITING	KEY	WIRE	YELLOW	
YES	EDGE	MEMORY	SELF	YEAR		WORM	YOUNG	

of such general utility that it is better to have them on the list. Lastly come *may* and *will*, auxiliaries of possibility and permission, and of futurity.

All these words in Basic take all the inflections of full English. Thus *give* is a head word, under which might be listed in a full table *gives*, *gave*, *giving*, and *given*. This raises puzzling questions as to how words are to be counted. If we list all the inflections of a verb, just when do we stop ? Do we list *kept* in " I kept it " and " It was kept " as two separate entries, though they are the same in form ? We would probably list *put* in " I put it here now " and " I put it there yesterday " as two, if we listed *give* and *gave* separately. But then, since " I am," " You are," and " He is " use different forms, why not list *give* five times to correspond with *I*, *you*, *you* (plural), *we*, *they*—adding another two entries for the imperative and the infinitive ? Similar quandaries arise in counting the pronouns. Ogden listed *I*, *he*, *you* and left it at that, knowing well that a one-page list of head words would not be the place where an intelligent person would look for their plurals (*we you*, *they*) or for the neutral (*it*), the feminine (*she*), the accusatives, and the possessives (*him*, *her*, *it*, *his*, *her*, *its*, etc.). Similarly *who* covers *whom*, *whose*, *which*, and *what*. As with *more*, *most* which go with *much*, and *less*, *least*, he saw that a table of related forms was what the learner needed for such things. The Word List is not a manual of Basic, but the briefest, compactest possible specification of the language. I mention all these trivia because hostile critics of Basic have been very willing to take time out to complain about such points instead of consulting one of the texts (*The Basic Words* or *The ABC of Basic English*) which would at once have answered all their questions, and relieved their professed bewilderment. My reader must forgive me for taking time out here to answer them. There is in fact an expanded model of the Basic Word List which includes all forms under the 850 head words, including plurals of all nouns and all recommended compound words. (*undergo*, for example). But that is a comparatively unwieldy thing. It is hardly manageable by a printer and was in fact handmade in China, where all available copies remain. It is a good thing to hang on a classroom wall, but not so generally useful as Ogden's one-page summary.

The reduction of the verbs to eighteen was the key to the

discovery of Basic. It explains what otherwise would seem impossible : the vast covering power of such a mere handful of words. These " operators," in combination with other Basic words, translate adequately more than four thousand verbs of full English. And they do it sometimes with gain in force and clarity. We shall compare some examples later. The use of these words, in place of more learned-looking words, has for centuries been increasing for simple, colloquial, informal speech and writing. Students of the history of English knew, of course, that words like *make, take, put, get* and *give* had been extending their spheres of influence in the language, but no one before Ogden's demonstration realized how vast a domain these unobtrusive little words had won. Willing, serviceable little workers, they were less impressive than the more literary verbs, but handier and safer. We shall see in connection with the teaching of Basic how this translation works out. Here a few examples will suffice. People *inserted* and *extracted* less and less, *put in* and *took out* more and more. Followers of Dr. Johnson at his most characteristic might be reluctant to give up words like *abandon, abdicate, abjure, cede, desert, desist, forego, forsake . . . relinquish, renounce, resign, vacate, withdraw*, and *yield* in place of *give up*—their homely Basic rendering—but a public unblessed by and unprotected by a sound training in philology escaped multiple dangers. So did the language itself. Every language is under constant attack by the tongues of its less expert users. One has only to watch—in a Chinese university, for example—the degradation of such learned words, when used without awareness of their implications, to see that they need protection. Basic English, by providing invulnerable but adequate substitutes for these more delicate instruments, can serve our language as a fender. It can guard full English from those who will blur all its lines and blunt all its edges if they try to write and talk it before they have learned to read it.

Apart from the amazing power these words have to take over the work of other verbs, they are in themselves the most indispensable verbs of full English. They have to be learned and well learned anyhow by anyone learning English. By concentrating on them, Basic can teach them as no system that adds further verbs can.

Below the verbs in Column One come twenty words (*about* to *with*) whose peculiarity is that they handle positions and directions. Basic groups them together as " directives," separating them from the other preposition-adverbs for an interesting reason. All these much-used little words have, of course, a great variety of meanings in full English. In general the usefulness of a word and the variability of its uses go together, as we would expect. It is useful because it will do so many things. Naturally, the words best worth teaching will be the hardest to teach— unless you succeed in analysing and arranging their uses so that as far as possible the links between the meanings become obvious. If you can do that, these words in a large measure teach themselves. This, it will be remembered, was my fourth point above. Ogden's analysis of the uses of these directives, and his separation of those that are intelligible (if taught in the right order) from those that are not, is perhaps the clearest example of this. As a contribution to the teaching of English (Basic or full) it is second only to his " break-down " of the verb.

In their central uses—those to be taught first—all these twenty words have to do with position or direction in *space*. In these uses they can all be illustrated in one diagram.

So presented this is obvious enough. But it is surprising how few teachers of English have used these physical senses in elucidating other uses of these words that are not physical. I suspect they have been daunted by the word " metaphor." And that is as though an engineer let himself be daunted by the word " stress." It is not suggested that teachers should explain the *theory* of metaphor to their classes. To teach that is no light undertaking. But if a series of examples is presented (leg of a man, leg of a dog, leg of a table) the connections between the uses of a word which metaphor has established become very easily apparent. The whole art of learning a language is in recognizing familiar features in new settings.

Of the other uses of these directive words, some are simple metaphors from these space senses, some are rather more complex metaphors going by steps, and some are irrational and incomprehensible accidents of the history of the language, and therefore cannot be understood and have to be just learned and remembered as brute facts. The important thing to do in teaching them is to separate and postpone these irrational " idioms " and give the others in the order that makes them most lucid and intelligible to the learner. Then he can see how and why the words do what they do in English.

Consider here the word *on*. " On the table," " on the wall," " on the earth," " on earth," " on Monday," " on view," " on

my mind," " on approval," " on a line," " on no account,"
" going on," " and so on."

Try out the effects of substituting *in* for *on* in a large collection
of such phrases. That brings out better than anything else what
the problem of teaching the indispensable words of English in
the most economical fashion is. I go further into the detail of all
this in a later chapter. Here the point is that it is possible to
choose a key sense for *on* and an order for the presentation of the
other uses that makes all those that are intelligible relatively easy
to master. In most pre-Basic teaching any and every use of *on*
which happened to turn up has been given equal attention.
Such hugger-mugger methods are wickedly wasteful of mental
energy, the most valuable commodity in the world.

A similar selective ordering of their uses has been given in
Basic to all its words. The recommendations are recorded in
The Basic Words. As a result, learning Basic, if these recommendations are followed, becomes a much lighter task than the learning
of the same 850 words in the full range of their senses taken at
random. But many who have thought they were studying
Basic seem hardly to have looked into *The Basic Words* or to be
aware as yet of the possibilities of economy that little book offers.

The rest of our tour of the Basic Word List can be made more
swiftly. The same principles apply throughout. Why any one
word appears on it depends on the absence of others. Occasional
overlaps (*boot, shoe ; sock, stocking* are the most conspicuous) are
explained by trade or other special customs. It must not be
forgotten that comprehensiveness is a prime aim, though no
one pretends or has ever pretended that any small set of words
can cover everything. What would the rest of the language be
doing if it could ! Nonetheless, the seeming omissions that for a
while puzzle most English-speaking persons who take up Basic
cease to be troublesome when the other words or phrases with
which the gap can be filled have been noticed. *Can* for example
is replaced through *possible, able to, let,* and *may*. Both *can* and *may*
are tricky words for a beginner in English. It is altogether best
to let him master *may* first. Then, if he is going on to the rest of
English, *can* will be an easier problem for him; similarly with
must, whose meanings are handled through *have to* and *necessary*.
In general in judging these decisions we should try to see them
with the eyes of a learner of English, rather than with a mind
that has full English at its disposal.

Among the six hundred names of things are many that at first

sight may be taken to be verbs: *act, attack, attempt, change, fall*, for
example. In Basic they are nouns. The powers of the operators
allow such words to be used in phrases that make a verb use
of them unnecessary. Thus in Basic we do not *act* in any of the
confusing senses of that verb, but we may *take* the part of Hamlet
in the play. In general we *do* whatever it is. Again, in Basic we
do not *attempt* something or *attack* someone, we *make* an attempt
or an attack; we do not *change* things, we *make* changes in them ;
we do not *fall*, we *have* a fall, and so on. But these indications
would be misleading unless I point out at once that Basic, through
the rule summarized by "derivatives in -er, -ing, and -ed from
three hundred nouns," has many other ways of handling these
meanings. We may add -*er* to these words to give us the name
of the agent—the actor, attacker, and so on. With three of these
(*actor, creditor, sailor*) the spelling is -*or* and not -*er*. This 1 per
cent irregularity is not troublesome. To the same words we may
add -*ing*, to give us nouns for the action and corresponding
adjectives : " The acting was bad," " He is the acting manager,"
" He was acting in the manager's place." This is a far simpler
way of teaching these uses than through the nomenclature of
participles and gerunds—that bane of so many schoolchildren's
days. Similarly, we may add -*ed* to give us another adjective.
" The play was acted." This provides us with the past participles
and the passives of our three hundred words, without bringing
in the complexities of the full verb and the construing difficulties
it occasions (*see* pp. 50-51).

The application of this rule is in practice much simpler than
may appear. The meanings of the nouns, as they are taught
in Basic, really control the use of these endings when they are
needed. The list of the three hundred and a full discussion will
be found in *The ABC of Basic English*. As Ogden there notes
(p. 82) there are other words in the Basic List that take some of
these endings, and English speakers writing in Basic may use
them with due care. Whether they will be clear to learners
depends, of course, on the rest of the sentence and the occasion.

It is in connection with this rule that the charge has been
made that Basic creates " wholly unnecessary difficulties . . .
difficulties lacking in Standard English." This is wholly false.
The alleged difficulties are troubles only to an ankylotic grammarian viewing Basic from the standpoint of a complete knowledge
of English. They do not exist for the foreign learner. He does not
look on his task from that standpoint. He has not yet learned full

B

English. What the rule in fact does is to *postpone* difficulties until the learner is at a stage when they will be less of a threat to his progress.

This last point may be stressed. Rules such as this are formulated for the convenience of teachers and expositors. They are guides rather than drill sergeants. Unfortunately grammar is the subject that of all others arouses the most obstinate propensities in the human mind. It is not an accident that grammarians by tradition are furious and rage. The formulation of any rule is to them a professional challenge to argue hard cases regardless of whether the general advance of a learner is helped thereby or hindered. It is easy to forget what rules and system are for. Too many teachers fall into this oblivion likewise. Too often in language teaching it is as though we confused hairdressing with famine relief ; our pupils are starving for means of expression, and we spend our time combing away at their unruly syntax or erratic phonemes.

The other summarized rules on the Basic List, except the last, explain themselves. We add *s* to most of the nouns to make their plurals, but follow normal English custom in all the exceptions. We add -*ly* to the adjectives to form adverbs (*kind, kindly*), but make all the normal adjustments of spelling (*able, ably*). We form comparatives with *more* and *most*, but also, with short words, use -*er* and -*est* (*smaller* and *the smallest*). *Good* and *bad* take *better*, *best* and *worse, worst*. Questions follow normal practice and, as we have seen, all the forms of the operators and pronouns are used.

Finally comes a formula that has been the occasion for a considerable amount of misunderstanding. It concerns a point of general policy. Ogden, looking realistically at the learner's actual situation, the real difficulties of language learning as opposed to vocabulary assimilation, and the means of communication already available, recognized that the numbers, for example, are not in the same position as most other English words. The learner has the figures to use ; all he has to learn is how to spell and pronounce them. He has no subtleties or variations of meaning to deal with. Similarly, in a less degree, with the names of the days of the week and the months of the year. The calendar presents them better than any text that does not just reprint it. Again, the metric system is adopted by nineteen governments, current in other countries, and all but universal for science. Its English pronunciation is the only task that remains. The other measurement terms in English possess, also, scientific definiteness of meaning. But, alas, the actual measures employed vary distressingly from region to region, and from trade to trade. This was another reason for excluding them from a general-purposes list, a reason applying also to currency terms. The main argument, though, for making numerals and calendar, measurement and currency terms addenda to the Basic List is their specific notational character. In this they are like proper names or mathematical or chemical signs, rather than like the general run of the common nouns of the language. They belong essentially to the nomenclatures of the sciences.

In addition to these there are the international words mentioned in this rule. Basic at present recognizes fifty words as current in all parts of the world wherever there is some likelihood of anyone's needing them. Typical are *bar*, *piano*, *restaurant*, and *telephone*, the names of and some of the terms in the chief sciences, and titles such as *president*. They are used by Basic, but it would have been silly to include them as though they were a part of the language that has to be taught.

This brings me to a side of Basic which to many offers some of its most interesting possibilities : its use as a connecting frame work through which the language of science could become international. This promise which Basic presents has always had a very important place in Ogden's design. It is obviously absurd that anything that is so much the common concern of mankind as the advance of science should be held up, continually, by language barriers, if there is any way of overcoming them. Anyone aware, even in one field, of the amount of relevant data and suggestion, which is hidden from him merely by his inability to read effectively in enough languages, will feel this. It is felt most acutely by natives of the linguistically isolated countries. A scientific worker in Australia, Brazil, or China, if he is to keep " abreast of his subject," must, as a rule, equip himself to read effectively in three foreign languages. In the near future he may well have to add Russian as a fourth. By the time he has so equipped himself he is years behind his fortunate rivals in more polyglot centres. There is little need to stress the point except by adding that *effective* reading (as opposed to the vague reading which is one of the most damaging ways of wasting our time) is harder to achieve, in view of the manner in which even very important papers are commonly written, than is

currently assumed. If there is a way of avoiding these frustrations
we should give it our best attention.

Ogden has recently published a report on the progress of Basic
toward a solution of these difficulties in the volume *Basic for
Science* which supersedes the earlier *Basic English Applied : Science*
(1931). It is written in Basic, and for the scientifically minded
would be the most suitable example of Basic writing to examine.
It is documented with specimens of the use of Basic, ranging
from popular expositions to abstracts of advanced research. It
contains also a representative selection from the forthcoming
Basic Science Dictionary, and the latest forms of the short lists of
scientific terms which enable a proficient in Basic to write for
students conversant with a science but limited in their English.

Clearly enough, such students do not require a full mastery
even of Basic before being able to profit from such writings.
The technical terms of their subject replace for them many everyday words which a novel in Basic, for example, is likely to employ.
What they do need is familiarity and ease with the Basic constructions and with the words that are most useful in explanations, in
accounts of procedure, and in describing causal and other
relations. They do not get this from ordinary courses in English
until a very late stage. Basic, from the very fact that it econo-
mizes in its words and uses a defining description where a
larger language would use some special word brought in for the
purpose, gives training in this sort of language almost from the
start.

We may therefore hope that the slow progress toward the
internationalization of the nomenclatures of the sciences, halted
by the wars, will gain fresh impetus as it is realized that Basic
English supplies the framework through which the vast vocabularies of science and technology could operate supranationally.
The transportation, as it were, is ready and waiting—all that
has to be done is to regularize the verbal packings of the already
standardized goods that have to be interchanged.

But Basic has done much more in this scientific field than
" stand and wait." A Basic Science Library—" a programme of
science in Basic designed for the general reader, the learner of
English, and the teaching of science in schools "—has been
assembled as a nucleus for further developments. The first of
them, *A Basic Astronomy*, appeared in 1934, and a version of
Faraday's *The Chemical History of a Candle*, two selections from the
writings of J. B. S. Haldane, *Science and Well-Being* and *The Outlook*

of Science made by William Empson, and *Living Things* an introduction to biology by J. W. N. Sullivan, followed. More recent examples are H. S. Hatfield's *European Science*, *What Things Are Made of* and *Inventions and Their Uses in Science To-day*, and A. P. Rossiter's *The Growth of Science*. The last two have reached a large public through becoming " Pelican Specials " issued by Penguin Books.

Those who know what an utter dearth of serious, intellectually mature reading matter in linguistically simple form is encountered by every student of English from China to Peru will best understand what even these beginnings can accomplish. They fit into the school and college programmes of those who are learning English as an aid to their work in science, but they are by no means limited to that use. In China—to speak of the foreign conditions I know best—the main incentive behind the learning of English is interest in what is most distinctive about the West, its science. And a school programme in English cannot begin to feed this curiosity with information and suggestions too early. In the teaching texts produced by the Orthological Institute of China, the elementary physiology of breathing and nutrition and the essentials of hygiene are taken up as early as the Second Book, before the students have got much more than halfway through the 850 words. That is what the selection of those words makes possible. Anyone who has some such special field in view can begin work on it without waiting for the whole Basic vocabulary to be assimilated, or even for the introduction of all the Basic constructions. The teaching of the remainder can well be combined with study of important subject matter. This is not the least of the enormous advantages, as to motivation, possessed by Basic.

This flexibility of Basic, which comes from the reduction of the verb and the separation of the structural operation words from the content vocabulary, is what I should finally stress in this chapter. Many critics who went not much further in their preliminary study than a glance over the Word List, and who supposed that anything that they did not immediately understand about the system must be a blunder, have complained of its rigidity. I go into one source of this mistake in the fourth chapter. Basic has, in fact, through its supplementary lists of words—lists for science, for economics, for the study of English poetry, for the Bible—arranged things so that special interests should be able to develop themselves at the earliest possible moment through Basic. One hundred and fifty extra nouns and adjectives permit a very dignified and faithful new translation of the Bible (*see* Appendix). In practice they take over the work of much the same number of words of less Biblical use. As aids to informed reading of it are *The Bible : What It Is and What Is in It* by E. Evans and T. H. Robinson, and *African Beliefs and Christian Faith* by Edwin W. Smith. Again, students who wish to get to Shakespeare's English as quickly as possible will find the text of his *Julius Cæsar* printed opposite a version in Basic English, with elaborate glosses, information on his language, and background materials in Basic in the footnotes.[2]   There are also available in Basic the passages from Plutarch from which Shakespeare worked. In yet a third direction, students who wish to enlarge their English constructions beyond those of Basic, by passing gradually to the free use of verbs, will find the way prepared in my abridged version of Plato's *Republic,* where verbs parallel to nouns in Basic (*to change, to know,* etc.) are put to work.   A version of Plato's *Meno,* made in strict Basic by J. Rantz, might be used as an introduction to the Platonic themes.

In these and other ways, Basic goes out to meet the needs of diverse people. It by no means stays cribbed and confined within its defensive stronghold of 850 proud words, as some ill-informed persons have alleged. It will be agreed, I think, that even the sketch I have given here shows evidence of the catholicity of Basic, its readiness to take due regard of different interests and purposes. With a main stress on science, it still gives the world its most universally readable Bible, and its experimental versions of other great books are from Shakespeare and Plato. The other items on its book list will confirm this impression. All these are first fruits. I think they show, to those who read them, that the tree was of good stock and well planted and that Basic has begun to put the materials and techniques for a common culture before the world.

I am making no attempt to sketch the history of the spread of Basic through its first ten years. The war interrupted too many promising starts—in China, Japan, Czechoslovakia, Denmark, Greece, to mention only a few instances—and it has put too

[2]For suggestions on uses of this text in the English classroom, see " On Teaching Shakespeare," by Christine Gibson, *The English Journal,* September, 1942.

many obstacles in the way of communications with other countries, too many of the best workers have been diverted by war needs, and curtailments due to the war have interfered with too many developments for any adequate up-to-date presentation to be possible. This is no moment for a historical summary. Thanks in a large measure to support from the Rockefeller Foundation and the Payne Fund, more progress has been made than anyone with a realistic awareness of the difficulties such a radical innovation in language teaching must encounter can readily believe. Basic is not among the casualties of the war. As that supreme demonstration of our need for a wider general culture and for clearer exchanges of man's better ideas was spread over the planet, Basic enterprises suffered along with so many other attempts toward a more reasonable future. The frustration is temporary ; essential work has continued—though not as it would have done in a peaceful world. When the time comes, the necessary materials and instrumentalities will be found ready.

Chapter Three

THE SIMPLIFICATION OF ENGLISH

WHY ANY language should in the course of its growth turn toward analysis is a question on which theoretical linguistics to-day will hazard only conjectures. By " analysis " no more is meant here than the process of breaking down the meaning carried, for example, by the word *accompany* into the separated meanings carried by the words *go in the company of*, or the meaning of *hinder* into the meanings of *get in the way of*. Analysis itself might here be phrased as *giving in separate words*. Most languages analyse to some degree, but in some—English is the outstanding example—analysis becomes a dominant tendency, spreading nearly everywhere, replacing, characteristically, verb inflections by separated auxiliary verbs and cases by prepositional phrases. And along with these syntactic changes goes a habit (in English at least) of paralleling less analytic expressions (*ascend* and *descend*, for example) with phrases which give, as it were, a dissection of their meaning in terms of separated components.

English has developed its habits of analysis very far, and in so doing has made a Basic English possible. It is tempting to connect these developments with a taste for common-sense philosophy in speakers of English, a popular inclination to inquire realistically into the meanings of long or scholarly-looking words. But similar words are not felt to be " scholarly " by speakers of other languages ; and perhaps it is the very existence of the analytic expressions that makes us regard the word with more condensed meaning as belonging to a more formal mode of the language.

This differentiation between learned and market-place English may well be a result, in part, of the invasions, warlike and pacific, which England underwent in the chief formative period of the language. The Danes found Angles in possession. Two peoples, largely unlettered, talking two remarkably similar languages, rubbed as it were, their everyday expressions, together. In talking to one another, Danes and Englishmen had no feeling that one was any better than the other. They were equals. So there was much give and take, exchange and adjustment, between the two languages. If a Dane got the sense of what the Englishman was saying, the smaller details of his ways of saying it were not important. The outcome was that in the parts of England in which most of the Danes were living, the development of the language, the process of smoothing and levelling out the forms of "grammar" went on specially quickly. Most important, as Jespersen has said in his *Growth and Structure of the English Language* : " It is precisely the indispensable elements of the language that have undergone the strongest Scandinavian influence, and this is raised into certainty when we discover that a certain number of those grammatical words, the small coin of language . . . which are nowhere else transferred from one language to another, have been taken over from Danish into English."

At a certain point on this page I again went over into Basic. Let me now put these observations of Jespersen into Basic, not necessarily to make them any clearer but so that the reader may see how that is done : " In fact, the most necessary parts of the language are the very ones on which the effect of Scandinavian languages has been greatest. We become certain of this when we see that a number of working or structure words, the small change of language, have been taken into English from the Danish. There is no other example of such words being taken over from one language to another." From " In talking . . ." to this point I have been using Basic.

This rubbing together of the two languages, we may imagine, wore off many inflections—the removable points of variance— and at the same time it stretched the range of service of those little " all-purpose " verbs—*give, get, put take, have, make*, etc.— which are the mainspring of Basic English. This at least would be a comprehensible picture, though it should not be taken too seriously as linguistic history. Data for deciding what actually took place are lacking. However it happened, English did develop a language within the language—a very powerful and comprehensive means of analytic expression due largely to the phrase-making capacities of these verbs.

This smoothing out of English grammar, so happily begun by the Danes, was continued through an extraordinary series of linguistic accidents. Simple language most needs protecting from the scholar and the grammarian. Fortunately, through the formative period of our language, " grammar " meant Latin grammar. Until modern times purists were kept harmlessly busy with the learned parts of the language.

The next great invasion of Britain, the Norman, gave English

B*

a court language, intellectual, fashionable, and fine, and many
terms of cookery, morals, and sport, but it hardly touched the
common speech—the " indispensable elements of the language."
And while the upper-class English were learning French, the
rest were teaching English to the followers of the Norman lords.
Once again in this process the grammatical twists were being
straightened ; the most generally useful parts of the language
were being developed—undisturbed by the attentions of the
learned.

Young children apparently do not mind how hard a language
is. They can jump from learning Chinese to learning German
without seeming to notice much difference. A child's mind is a
sort of verbal flypaper. It is otherwise, alas, with us adults. A
richly inflected language—teeming with case and mood and
tense and gender forms—is very much harder for the adult to
learn than a relatively uninflected language like English, which
does its grammatical work almost entirely through word order.
English became simple largely through being taught to so many
adult aliens in the historical period when it was most ductile and
malleable.   Millions of tough, blunt minds have done their
best to make a dent in it. No other language—Chinese, perhaps,
apart—has had such a hammering.   And this process has been
continued on this continent :   " Destination ?   Occupation ?
Relatives ?" the immigration officer asks.   " Where are you
going ? What work do you do ? Are any of your family here ? "
someone behind the immigrant translates automatically into
Basic. It is no accident that English has a Basic form. A thousand
years of teaching it out of school have gone into its making. No
other European language has been forced through the same
development. A French, Spanish, or German equal in range and
power to Basic English would require something over two
thousand words, while the necessary grammatical rules, if the
usages of the parent language were not to be violated, would be
vastly more complex. So we may not hope for a comparable
Basic Spanish or Portuguese to help us in our hemispheric communications, much though the task of learning those languages
might be lightened through attempts to produce simplified forms.

Basic English, then, when Ogden took up the detail of his
research in 1926, was a possibility prepared by the history of the
language. It was present in scattered form among the inexhaust-
ible resources of English, but it needed to be disengaged, extracted

assembled and systematized before it could be available either
as a quasi-independent medium of communication or as the
right introduction to the rest of English. On the details and
the principles of this very extensive task of selection and organization much has been written by Ogden and others, and an
outline was presented in Chapter Two. To go over it comprehensively is no part of our purpose here. Much of it is a matter
for specialists. The techniques are of interest chiefly to those
who have similar work in view. The arguments for and against
particular decisions, at this or that point in the systematization,
are necessarily both extensive and subtle. They are made more
difficult because inevitably each depends in large degree upon
the decisions taken upon other points. As with any other complex design, we cannot easily isolate single features for separate
consideration. We have to envisage as comprehensively as we
can the working of the whole machine.

It will be, therefore, with the outcomes as a whole that we
shall be chiefly concerned, with the primary aims of Basic English
and the principal means by which it attains them. The minutiæ,
which in so large an undertaking must be many, will be left aside.

The primary aims are themselves highly interrelated. They
may be summarized as follows : to provide a minimum form of
normal English, with the amplest *covering power* and the highest
discriminative capacity compatible with the *greatest ease* in learning.
This formulation brings out the interdependence of these aims
and suggests how the design had constantly to balance rival
advantages. It would have been relatively easy, for example, to
work toward a short word list with widest covering power, if
the accuracy with which ideas expressed in full English could
be rendered were a minor consideration. Again, by sacrificing
covering power, by resting content with a language fitted for
trade, for example, but unable to handle science or political
theory, it would have been easier to include more specific terms
for commodities. Yet again, a larger vocabulary would have
allowed increased covering power and discrimination to be
attained—but at the price of a heavier learning load.

This last point is more important than it may seem. Many
have wondered why Ogden set the numerical limits of Basic
where he did—at about the number of words that can be printed
clearly on one side of a sheet of business notepaper. But, as I
have insisted above, the weight, to the learner, of a word list is
not simply proportional to its length. At many points in a

learner's progress additional words do not merely *add* to his task ; they *multiply* it. They increase the probability of confusion as to their senses, as to their grammatical functions, as to their pronunciation, and as to their spelling. There are a number of well-marked landing stages in the beginner's ascent, points at which his further advance will be greatly eased, if he ceases, for a while, to take in more vocabulary and new constructions. He should devote himself instead to the cultivation of his command of those he has already acquired. When he is solidly established in his handling of these, he can go on to new vocabulary and new constructions with very much less risk of having the old patterns disturbed by the new. Neglect of this fact—a too rapid and too unregulated advance into new forms, which are therefore never properly understood—is the chief cause of broken English, a developmental disease which is, alas, in most instances incurable.

Among these landing stages one of the most important occurs at about the point to which Basic English leads the learner. It is the first point at which he has a stock of English words that can, between them, cover most of the ideas and interests upon which he may wish to communicate. It is the first point at which he has a sufficient supply of grammatical forms with which to manipulate his vocabulary so that it will develop and exert its range of meanings. Some of its words, of course, will not happen to chime in with any one learner's range of concerns. These will be different words for different learners, and any one learner may rightly neglect words that do not serve his purposes. But the Basic Word List is the briefest which permits books, articles, radio talks, letters, etc., covering all topics to be composed for learners in general without sending them back to a bilingual dictionary. And similarly the syntax taught in Basic English is the simplest syntax which permits these words to be ordered in a fully expressive and sufficiently supple fashion (see *Word Economy* by L. W. Lockhart).

One consideration had to be dominant throughout the designing of Basic English—the consideration that it must use only normal English sentence patterns. It would have been easy to have relaxed this condition and allowed sentence forms which though non-English are not in themselves ambiguous. Chinese, for example, dispenses with plural forms for nouns without resultant confusion. English does so in rare, exceptional instances, as with *sheep* and, conversely, *scissors* (to quote the two Basic examples). Getting plural endings right, as every teacher knows, gives the learner a considerable amount of trouble. Nonetheless, Basic, holding fast to its often repeated principle, " If it is bad English, it is bad Basic," insists upon normal English practice here, and forbids " two man " and " three boy," as it forbids " the sheeps " and " the scissor." Chinese again disregards gender in its pronouns and uses *t'a* when English says *he, she* and *it*. Basic English keeps to the three distinct forms of normal English. Some economy of learning effort might be made by letting *it* serve all three purposes. But here, we may suspect, there would be a price to pay in ambiguity. In the early days of Basic English, an enthusiast for simplification did, in fact, recommend the use of *it* as a universal pronoun. He coupled this with an appeal for the discontinuance of the English *aspirate*—in the interests of German and other learners who find the English *h's* difficult to manage. Ogden was able to point out that a type sentence could then take the form, " It it it," which might mean " He hit her," " She hit him," " It hit it," and the rest! *Hit* was in the enthusiast's list. It is not in Basic.

These are but random samples of the numerous simplifications of standard English forms that might, in varying degrees, lighten a learner's task—at the cost of departure from current English " good usage." It is interesting to play, for a moment, with some other possibilities that would simplify English accidence without resulting in anything worse than archaic or dialect English. One of these would be the dropping of our verb inflections. We manage the future with *will* ; we could manage the past with *did*. Again, the present tense of *be* could be standardized without loss of clarity : *I be here, You be there, He be there, They be there; He will be there, He did be there* would be the outcome. So, too, with all third persons singular : *He do* looks unlettered, though it is a very creditable regularization. " This lamentable and unmannerly hissing about a third person," Ogden notes, " has been characterized by Sir Richard Paget as un-English. It would probably have disappeared long ago in the normal course of events had not printers, lexicographers and schoolmasters rallied so egregiously to its defence ; and if any reform is overdue in our accidence, here is surely an appropriate casualty."[1]

Nonetheless, few will doubt that Ogden was well advised in resisting all such temptations. Every departure would have

[1] *Basic English and Grammatical Reform*, p. 7.

meant something to be *unlearned* if the student wished to proceed to a more comprehensive knowledge of English. And there is nothing in Basic that a student has to unlearn. Some have questioned this, who did not know much about Basic. It has even been asserted that Basic " cannot be expanded into real English." The writer omitted to say why not or why Basic is not " real English." However, he added that " confined to its proper purposes, Basic may have a useful function to play in promoting the expansion of real English," so the reader can decide how seriously he will take him. In fact, well-written Basic is as real as any other English, and there is no special difficulty of any sort in passing on from Basic to the rest of English. No language can be taught as a whole in a flash. There have to be steps and stages in the learning process, and it is one of the greater advantages of Basic, an outcome of its scope, that the advance to more complete English can be so solidly grounded on and carried through by means of explanations in Basic. The dangers of the bilingual pocket dictionary and misleading identifications with expressions in the other language are thus avoided.

Every learner of any language, of course, discovers, as he goes on, that more things are possible in the language than he supposed. While we advance we are endlessly modifying our conceptions of its structural resources. But expanding our knowledge, if it does mean giving up some oversimple notions, is not an unlearning of things taught. Early views must be incomplete. They are not, therefore, incorrect as far as they go. On any informed view of usage Ogden held fast to the principle that there must be nothing in Basic that anyone would have to unlearn.[2] The disadvantages of that would outweigh any gains in ease of learning. And, in view of the close relations between

[2]The worst offence in Basic against custom is in connection with the prefix *un* before quality words. Here is Ogden's comment : " A certain number of these formations, e.g., *unregular*, *unprobable*, are departures from standard English. All, however, can readily be avoided by the use of *not*, and the beginner who desires not to disturb the susceptibilities of the purist during the next few years can thus always attain his desire. Otherwise, the justification for these innovations is that while they develop a salutary tendency in the language they are too inoffensive to shock very deeply " (*Basic English*, p. 52). In classroom practice, *not regular*, *not possible*, etc., are taught. *Unregular*, etc., if and when they appear, will be treated at the teacher's discretion as circumstances direct. Let purists complain if they will !

a simplified language and the full language which were discussed
in Chapter One, there is ground for thinking this decision
doubly wise. It safeguards the learner's future interest in the
rest of the language and at the same time it protects the language
itself from corruption. A world language, after all, will be
written and talked by many more foreign than native users.
At the best, as we saw, there will be a considerable strain upon
its structure. For this reason the solid simplicity of the normal
English constructions used in Basic has an added importance.
They are, on the evidence of history, such as best resist distortion.

Here, while radical simplifications are our topic, will be the
place to touch upon simplification of spelling. It would certainly
be a great advantage if an authoritative system of regularized
spelling were adopted for English. On the other hand, such a
reform would tend to fix English pronunciation at a moment
in its history when its conventionally approved sounds are—
as Robert Bridges insisted—not at their best. Moreover, rival
American-British pronunciations might become bones of contention. However that might be, the vexations which anomalies
of our spelling cause the foreign learner decrease rapidly as the
rate of his intake of new words falls off. In a small list, singu-
larities of spelling may in some cases even be an aid to recognition.
But clearly, in choosing the Basic words, regularity of the written
form could only be a minor factor, subordinate to more important considerations. So, too, with avoidance of homonyms—
though this, in part, accounts for the avoidance of *piece* (cf. *peace*)
and entered into some other decisions. On the whole, though
fanatics of reformed spelling have upbraided him for it, Ogden
did well to avoid the profound prejudices which innovations in
spelling, however reasonable, always excite. He had enough
entrenched obstructionism to break down when introducing
Basic, without opening a second and even more bitterly defended
front.

English was potentially simple when Ogden took up his task—
which was to make it actually and practically simple. It may be
well to consider for a moment what we should mean here by
" simple." Things that are simple to use are not necessarily
simple in themselves. We are becoming more and more familiar
with mechanisms—the typewriter, the radio, the automobile—
that are simple in use ; that is, easy to use effectively because of
complexities in their design introduced precisely to make them

so. An electric shaver can be simpler to use than an old-fashioned cut-throat razor. It is incomparably less simple in construction.

In appraising the simplicity of a language we have to keep our eye on the number of things a learner has to know ; that is, has to be able to do, if he is to use it successfully. These are our concern, rather than any facts of structure. By simplifying the grammatical structure of a language too far we can easily make it unworkable. Classical Chinese, for example, dispensed to an extreme degree with grammar. To take its place a tradition of interpretation was needed consisting largely of comparisons with instances of other uses of its phrases. A student has to be deeply read in the classics before he can interpret any passage with security. This gives classical Chinese a peculiar unity, but it makes the path of the beginning student extraordinarily hard.

We shall do well throughout to distinguish the things we have to be able to do from the accounts we give of how we do them. Walking is simple enough to those who can do it. But an adequate account of how we walk would overstrain any anatomist's or brain specialist's knowledge. The test of the simplicity of a language—in the sense that concerns us here— is not any theoretical account but *how easy it is to learn and use.* And that is something which only experience can determine. In the present state of our knowledge of theoretical linguistics, accounts of how a language works (which grammar attempts to supply) give us only very rough indications of the ease with which it may be learned and used. Of course, in extreme cases we can be sure that certain constructions in a language will make for difficulty, though even then we shall be wise to consider the whole language if we can. Thus a very highly inflected language equipped with numerous genders will be harder to learn, we may be sure, than an analytic, inflectionless language without genders. Even so we may again remember classical Chinese. If you strip a language of grammatical devices too far, you get sentences that might mean far too many different things.

In general a language that is easy to learn and use need not be simple in itself. It is only those things about it which the user has to adjust consciously and deliberately that need to be simple. We should find, if we attempted to carry an account of the grammatical structure of Basic English as far as possible, that it became extremely complex. But very little of that account would be useful to the learner. Only the parts of it that he needs to control deliberately in his practice concern him. And accordingly only those parts are relevant for us here. And, we may repeat, only the test of experience through teaching can show us which these are, and therefore which features of Basic English make the learner's path into it quick and smooth.

I shall confine myself in what follows to these. Relatively complete accounts of the grammar of Basic English and of the innovations in grammatical terminology convenient in describing it have been published by Ogden in *The ABC of Basic English*, which forms the Second Section of his *System of Basic English*. To this, and to his *Basic English and Grammatical Reform*, I shall refer any reader who requires more detail and a fuller examination of the inevitably difficult grammatical problems.

Those who wish to know in detail how Basic English may be taught in schools should consult one of the annotated teaching texts—either the Teachers' Edition of *The Basic Way to English*, or the Teachers' Edition of *Learning the English Language*, where fairly full recommendations will be found. Ogden's recommendations for learners not controlled by school routines are given in *Basic Step by Step*, to which, with *The ABC of Basic English*, reference should be made. This last is *not* for classroom use, a point that needs stressing. Many of the most persistent objections made to Basic have depended upon the supposition that it is a general teaching text. Translations into Japanese, German, French, and Swedish have appeared and others are in preparation. *Basic Step by Step*, which is a beginner's text, has been adapted for Russian, German, Spanish, French, Dutch, Polish, Norwegian, and other languages. Here we keep to the broad reasons why the learning of Basic English is so much easier than the learning of any other language, or section of a language, of comparable scope.

The most obvious feature is, of course, the limitation of the number of words. But a mere comparison of *the number* of words in Basic with *the number* of words in some other limited word list would not bring the chief point out. We should have to ask, further, what sorts of words they are. Words differ immensely in the ease with which we may learn to use them. The easiest words are names. They present the minimum of grammatical trouble. Next come adjectives : their positions with respect to the nouns they qualify can cause trouble. This trouble in English is reduced to a minimum by the general rule, in English prose, that the adjective comes before its noun ; or, in the predicative use, after the appropriate part of the verb *to be : the deep waters are cold*, not *cold are the waters deep*, except in poetic utterance. More difficult than the adjectives are some of the adverbs, as the trouble most of us experience with the placing of *only* will illustrate.

Opinions will differ as to which of the other sorts of words are most difficult. Teachers agree, on the whole, that verbs are the hardest, and next to them prepositions. But this judgment depends in a large measure upon the proportion such words bear to the other words taught. If there were many words in English that were as tricky as the articles *a* and *the*, articles might have a good claim to bad eminence among the vocables. As there are only two of them, the teacher, thankful for that mercy, does not rank them with the verb as among her major troubles. Verbs are difficult partly because of their inflections, partly because of the occurrence of irregularities among these inflections, and still more because of the very important part that verbs take in the construction of the sentence. The job of construing a sentence—of making out what its construction is—largely turns on recognizing the verb and on recognizing its form and the work it is doing. Thus, other things being equal, a language that contains few verbs will be easier to construe, and easier to express oneself in, than a language containing more verbs.

This has brought us to the greatest of the advantages that Basic English has over other languages. Its verbs are only eighteen. This means in practice three things :

1. From a very early stage in the study of Basic there is never any doubt as to which word in a sentence is the verb. If at an early point in his progress a learner meets, say, the word *change* in a sentence and has as yet no more than dim memories of sentences such as " All change at Dover," "I have no change," " What changes we see ! " and " That changes everything " to guide him, he inevitably runs into much needless uncertainty and risk of confusion.

Such examples are of course artificial, but complex English offers innumerable occasions for such mistakes to the learner who has not had much instructive experience of the language. So the limitation of the verbs to a very few, which because they are so few incessantly recur in his use of the language, gives a clarity and ease to his construing which is not to be measured merely in numerical terms. If at this stage we treble the number of our verbs and let them be verbs that might, as far as form goes, be nouns (singular or plural) we make construing far more than three times as hard for him. And with that we heighten the difficulty for him of innumerable other points in the behaviour of words other than verbs. We confuse him as to plurals while blurring his sense of the significance of the hiss or buzz that means " third person, singular, of the present." The old catch, " Time flies ! We cannot. They go too fast," illustrates this point very clearly. Worse still, we lead him in the most damaging fashion to think that utterly non-English constructions are somehow possible. We give him unnecessary excuses to suppose that combinations of words make sense which a more experienced eye would see at once as grammatically impossible in English.

2. One or more of the eighteen verbs will appear in every sentence. These repetitions stamp in their inflections as nothing else will. The changes of the irregular verbs are the really troublesome inflections in English. Continual practice is by far the most effective way of learning them. Of Basic verbs, *seem* is regular and provides a pattern for regular verbs to be learned later. The rest are irregular—in representative fashions. And they are the verbs which in any normal form of English do the most work. Mastery of their inflections —*give, gave ; get, got ; take, took*, etc.—is something never achieved by many learners who otherwise become fairly proficient in English. The learner of Basic has the very best chance of mastering them from the start, while his attention to them is relatively undistracted. Competitive patterns are reduced to a minimum.

3. More important, the varying meanings and implications of these key verbs in their chief combinations become established through the intensive practice which Basic enforces, far more firmly and fully than would be possible if they were introduced along with some miscellaneous scores of other verbs—as has been the custom in traditional school courses. The more we realize how great the part is that these verbs play in everyday, unrestricted English, the more important this point will appear. These are the verbs the ordinary English speaker understands best, the verbs he uses when he most wants to explain something clearly and simply, when he most wants " to get down to facts " and see what he is really saying. Thus, the point deserves to be stressed that Basic gives the learner a uniquely intensive training in these key English verbs before he passes on—with increasing experience—to as much of the rest of the language as he needs. " Let first things come first," might well be the motto of this system. These verbs are first in importance in English. There is

no doubt whatsoever of that. Basic puts them first—in teaching order and in the intensity of their cultivation also. That is one of the grounds of its claim to lay the foundations of a knowledge of English well and truly.

It is sometimes said that the characteristic Basic phrases *to give up* (in place of *to abandon . . . yield*, etc.) or *to give out* (in place of *to exude, emit, announce, distribute*, etc., in some of their senses) must be harder for the learner than the replaced verbs. This is letting theory take the place of facts. It has proved otherwise in practice, and the job of the theorist now is to learn how Basic works, not to invent reasons why it should not work. Actually, if the words that make up these phrases have been properly taught, the phrases themselves in adequate contexts give little trouble ; and they have to be mastered in any case if the learner is ever to manage conversational English.

Next in difficulty to verbs come prepositions. Most of these are simple-looking little words, but to get them right is one of the hardest parts of the learner's task. The apparent vagaries of *at, on, in, off*, and *from* too often baffle even the acutest and most ardent student. The difficulty with these is not so much in their grammatical behaviour as in the subtlety with which they enter into phrases—the differences between *on my way* and *in my way*, between *on my mind* and *in my mind*, and between *in my view* and *on my view*, for example. It is true that they also present grammatical difficulties. When is *up* a preposition and when an adverb, is a typical problem. But if the uses of these words are introduced in a well-thought-out order (they are rarely) these difficulties will not greatly trouble a learner. They may tax the grammarian's skill—but that is another matter altogether.

Setting aside *of* and *for* for special treatment, Ogden listed twenty of these little words as having to do—in their central or *pedagogically* root uses—with directions or positions in space. The list is : *about, across, after, against, among, at, before, between, by, down, from, in, off, on, over, through, to, under, up* and *with*. In their central senses these words may be all displayed in such a diagram as was given on page 31. The foreign learner can there *see* with his eyes and his mind at once what these little, easily confused words mean in their essential senses. Of course, in calling these their root sense (as he often does) Ogden is not primarily talking of their etymology. He is pointing to the senses from which a full and clear understanding of their other senses can best be grown. They are root senses because from them the learner can best proceed to a study of their other meanings in phrases.

Let us now take up the central sense of *on*, and its metaphoric extensions. The central sense is touching or contact. When my finger is on a surface, it is touching the surface. *On* very frequently carries two implications due to gravity. What usually keeps one thing on another? The other is under it and holding it up. When a book is on the table, or on a shelf, it is over the table (or shelf) and supported by it. So we add " over and supported by " as natural implications. But when a fly is on the ceiling, we leave out the " over it " implication and keep only " held up, dependent on " as a second ingredient reinforcing " touching." And when my finger is on my lips, only touching remains.

Now how may we use this analysis to put some of the metaphoric senses of *on* into intelligible order? In " on paper," " on the blackboard," " on the wall," the reference to contact with planes is clear. The words on paper or on the blackboard, and the picture on the wall are also supported by the surfaces they touch. So, too, with a bead that is on a thread. But how about a store that is on a certain street; or a town that is on my way? Here the store and the town are in contact with the line that is the street or my route. The meaning contrasts sharply with that of a car that is in the street or a town that is in a state. *In* has, as its central meaning, " enclosure, surrounded by "; and this contrast may be used to clarify " on my mind " and " in my mind " and the others of a preceding page. When I have something *on* my mind, it is like a weight pressing on me. The suggestion is painful. But it may be a pleasure to have it *in* my mind. It has then, as a rule, been encompassed if not assimilated, but what is *on* my mind is a problem still to be dealt with. Contrariwise, when something is " on my way," that is convenient; but when it is " in my way," it is an obstruction; it takes up some of the space through which I have to go. Again, compare " In my view, Mr. X is the criminal " with " On my view, Mr. X did it." *In* makes the guilt of Mr. X part of my view; it is surrounded by the considerations that together make up my opinion. But *on*, here, suggests a hypothesis, a set of assumptions that would support those conclusions did we make them, a framework on which we put the suggestion of X's guilt to see how it seems to us. This last is, of course, a subtler distinction, depending far more delicately upon context, and is not part of elementary English—though the parallel with " on my mind," " in my mind " is noticeable. As with all such refinements, we must not suppose the meanings of the phrases to be fixed for all occasions. They are not formulas to be collected and tucked away in a mental file. They are opportunities for the words to exert their powers, and it is the powers, the central meanings of the words, which the learner has to be led to understand by a suitable series of examples.

It will be seen from this sketch of the different sorts of words and the troubles they present to a learner, how far the difficulty of a language is from being simply proportioned to the *number* of words it requires him to memorize. Of two word lists, that is the simpler which contains the least number of troublemakers. Ogden has separated the troublemakers on the Basic Word List and set them together in its first column. The other seven and a half columns of nouns and adjectives hardly amount, together, to as hard a task for the learner as this first hundred words. But in calling them the first hundred I am referring merely to their place in the first column of the list. No one would suggest that all these words should be taught first, or many of them very early. Just which should come where in a teaching text and what the emphasis put upon them should be in comparison with the others is in fact a highly discussible pedagogic question—which is touched on in a following chapter. In any case it is clear that in several respects these words are in a different position from nouns and adjectives. It will further clarify our conception of what simplification entails if we consider some of these respects briefly.

In the first place there is virtual unanimity as to the necessity of including these one hundred words in any short list, whatever the principles on which the list is compiled. Whether we are content, as with the early word counts of E. L. Thorndike or Ernest Horn, to determine which words occur most frequently in various types of writing and base our list on frequency and range (the number of different sources using the word), or whether, as with Ogden's work, we take vastly more complex considerations into account, there is no substantial difference in the result as regards these one hundred operation or structure words. In the most recent and elaborate comparative study of these word lists,[3] a table displays the amount of overlapping between them for the different categories of words used in the Basic Word List. It shows that Ogden's one hundred operation words all appear in Thorndike's first thousand words (all but six of them in his first five hundred). After these comparisons the conclusion of the authors is, " The separation of the ' operations' from the rest of the vocabulary as is done in Basic English seems to us a fundamentally important contribution to the solution of this problem of teaching a foreign language " (p. 89). As study of the work done on such word lists since the publication of the Basic List shows, this aspect of Ogden's treatment has already radically affected the handling of the problem, though other aspects hardly less important may need more time before they are widely appreciated.

The most important part of his treatment is the inclusion of the verb-operators of Basic among these structural words. This has been recognized. " It seems linguistically sound too," Fries and Traver continue, " to include among these ' operators ' whatever *verbs* are used in a list for the first approach to English as a foreign language. The verb is a means of ' relating ' just as much as are adverb-prepositions and conjunctions. To classify the verb as an ' operator ' and therefore to use only a minimum number of verbs in a *first* vocabulary seems not only theoretically sound but helpful from a practical point of view " (p. 90).

By using the *Oxford English Dictionary* and counting the " distinct meanings " of words there given, Fries and Traver found for the Basic words a total of 12,425 meanings. For 850 words taken from Thorndike's first thousand most frequent words (all the first 500 and 350 taken at random from the second 500), they found a total of 21,120 meanings. " The great difference between these totals," they note, " seems to be due largely to the fact that Thorndike's list contains many verbs and the Basic List only the eighteen chosen as operators. If these figures have any significance, the learning weight of a list with verbs as vocabulary units is considerably greater than that of a list in which the verbs are reduced to a minimum number of operators " (p. 90).

[3] *English Word Lists : A Study of Their Adaptability for Instruction*, prepared for the Committee on Modern Languages of the American Council on Education by Charles C. Fries with the co-operation of A. Aileen Traver, 1940 (p. 74).

The significance of these figures—questionable though they are in themselves—is really far greater than the authors recognize. It was pointed out in Chapter Two that the words on the Basic List are by no means taught or used, *in Basic*, with all the " meanings " listed in the *Oxford English Dictionary*. Ogden and his co-workers were at great pains to limit the meanings recommended for the Basic words and to list the extensions and specializations they possess in Basic.   These limitations are specified in detail in *The Basic Words*. And it is odd that Fries and Traver should have overlooked them in this argument. If we take due account of them and of the fact that the covering power of Basic is nevertheless far greater than that of the 850 words from the Thorndike list, a relevant comparison proves vastly more to the advantage of Basic than such unanalysed figures can suggest.   The argument for the reduction of verb-operators to a minimum becomes, in fact, overwhelming.   It may be interesting, however, to note that this figure of 12,425 *Oxford English Dictionary* meanings for the Basic words given by Fries and Traver has been used by a hostile critic of Basic without any regard for these authors' conclusion from it.   Such is the technique of controversy.

" Meanings," of course, cannot be counted without a systematic method of deciding which " meanings " for a word are distinct, which not distinct, and when.   What matters, for the learner, is not whether two uses of a word are different but how they are connected, and how readily an understanding of one use leads to the understanding of others.   How many " uses " or " meanings " or " senses " we choose to say that a word has will depend, of course, upon how fine is the network of distinctions with which we analyse.   Any system for teaching English (or any other language) that avoids this problem builds upon quicksand.   The only thing to do is to face it and make a lexicographic analysis expressly for the purpose in hand.   Parallel to the choice of the recommended words, there has to be an ordered selection of senses (and extensions and specializations) for them. In fact, the two undertakings, if systematically carried through (as in *The Basic Words*) require and imply one another.   The simplification of vocabulary and the limitation and ordering of the meanings of every word in it are two branches of the same inquiry.   To profess, for example, to be " concerned with the simplification of teaching, not with the simplification of language "[4] is to forget the problem. That is the old and wasteful endeavour to teach English without deciding what English is to be taught. Every stage in a learner's advance represents some simplification of the language. The question is whether it is an intelligent and helpful simplification or not.

To return, however, to the contrasts between the operation words and the other words in Basic. Whereas there is this general agreement as to the choice of the structure words—with room, perhaps, for 1 per cent of reasonable difference in opinion—the choice of the remaining 750 is by no means on the same basis. Without these structure words an elementary English could not work or would not be a normal English. They are the necessary manipulative words of the language, its formal machinery—the others are the words it manipulates, the words that label and carry most of the content that the language has to handle. Most, but not all, for the structure words, the verbs especially, are by no means empty of content. Nonetheless the structure words are necessary in a way in which only a disputable portion of the others are. Even the most necessary of the other words are necessary in another manner.

The structure words are necessary because without them certain required forms of English sentences would not be possible. Content words are necessary because without them we could not talk about certain matters, or discuss certain ideas. The first is a formal necessity ; the last is a matter of practical convenience. Accordingly, the drawing up of a list of the structure words, and a recognition of its sufficiency and economy, called for one sort of talent—the drawing up of the rest of the list called for wider and different abilities. Whether you agree or not as to the list of structure words depends upon your grasp of essential English syntax and of the forms of thought that must be able to be expressed. Whether you agree or not as to the rest of the list depends partly upon your view of what the people using the language should be able to talk about, partly on your insight as to which words will best allow them to talk about as much of it as possible. It depends, too, upon the extent of your experience in making as few words as possible go as far as possible and yet be normal English. It depends, in fact, upon the skill and pertinacity of your experimentation with this problem.

[4] *The Interim Report on Vocabulary Selection*, London, P. S. King and Son, Ltd., 1936, p. 1.

A first answer supposes that the most necessary words will be the most frequent. Let us, therefore, count words and list those that appear most frequently. This plan does not work badly with the structure words. We should note, however, that the ten most frequent words (*the, of, and, to, a, in, that, it, is, I*)[5] are most frequent *because* they are most indispensable, not the other way around. High frequency suggests that the word may be important for a limited vocabulary. It does not *prove* that the word is necessary. Too many authorities on word frequencies have been far from clear on such points, and have too often argued from a word's frequency to its importance, as though other factors were of less consequence. Such a view always shows that the real problems of the undertaking have not been understood.

It is when we turn from the words of Column One to the nouns and adjectives that the necessity of distinguishing between the widest general-utility considerations and frequency considerations becomes evident. It is, of course, easiest—a great saving of reflection—to assume that nature and the habits of mankind have settled the matter and that the most used words must necessarily be the most useful ones. But, alas, in no department of human affairs is the most usual thing necessarily the thing of most use. And it is far from being so in language. The favourite adjective and the popular adverb, " fugacious as spring hats and parlour games," seem indispensable in their hour and tower up to giddy heights on the word-frequency counter's graph. Twenty-five years later they are as unfortunate for the foreigner who has acquired them as its date on an egg. The Bengal lawyer with his " Topping ! " and " Ripping ! " is only a shade more absurd than the Brazilian who has acquired his " absolutely " through a word-count recommendation.

Absolutely, for example, has been ranked as the 1,101st most frequent word in a compilation, representing a total of ten million word-occurrences. A student of verbal fashions could date the materials of the count from a few such facts. *Absolutely*, it will be noted, does no work that *very, certainly, completely, at all,*

[5] *These constitute* 25 per cent of the one hundred thousand running words counted in establishing their position. Ogden's *memoria technica* for these ten commonest English words (no more difficult, he suggests, than an announcement of " Maurice Farkoa in *Aren't We All ?* ") is *Theo Fandtoa in " That It Is I."*

and *quite* will not, in one way or another, do better. In all but a few contexts *absolutely* is an absolutely (*completely*) meaningless intensifier, adding nothing but emphasis. There is absolutely (*certainly*) no need for it in any limited word list. We can be absolutely (*very*) sure that our learner will never miss it. Isn't this true ? Absolutely ! (*quite ! certainly !* and *completely !*) We may note for contrast, however, that the adjective *absolute* has an important set of senses which *are* hard to represent with other words. The various oppositions of the absolute and the relative are the framework of all speculation from Parmenides to Einstein. It is interesting that one of the emptiest of adverbs should derive so from one of the fullest of adjectives. Go one step further, turn the word into a noun and *the Absolute* becomes the everything, or, if you prefer it so, nothing.

But to return to the choice of the simplest set of nouns and adjectives that together will cover the widest range of needs. Frequency has a minor, though important, role here. Other things being equal, if two equally desirable words cover much the same ground, the more frequent word is to be included. Obviously its higher frequency will make it more useful. And being heard and met with more often it will be more easily learned. On the other hand, having chosen it, we omit the other word, even though its frequency may be only slightly less, and very much higher than that of many other words. But we include these other words because without them great provinces of human concern would remain inexpressible.

Clearly for the choice of the words in this list there was needed a truly catholic and encyclopædic range of interests. Since all knowledge will be grist to this mill, since ideally our word list will be able to take *anything* that is said and rephrase it—as to its notional analysis—without damage to essentials, the quest for such a word list called for an extraordinary variety of general and particular awarenesses as well as for an extremely critical and discerning judgment in the use of English. And these gifts, in fact, came together for the task. It is not for nothing that Ogden's 1925 review[6] of the Encyclopedia Britannica was for years a collector's piece. Nor is it irrelevant that the editor of the International Library of Psychology and the History of Civilization should also have been creator and editor of *The Cambridge Magazine*, in its day the most exciting weekly in England—its

---

[6]It is now reprinted in Clifton Fadiman's *Reading I've Liked*.

pages packed with contributions by Hardy, Shaw, Bennett, Wells, and such ; nor that this seemingly academic polymath should be an active man of affairs with more varied dealings than anyone but himself ever knows, as well as a connoisseur of wide range (needing Hearst's resources to be an equally multifarious collector, but Ogden would know the least last thing about each of his acquisitions). Such a man's judgment on the utility of a word is not to be taken lightly. Nor is it irrelevant that he should be a psychologist who is also a wit— justly celebrated for the extravagance, the absurdity, and the mordancy of his flashes—nor that it is on language itself that he most triumphantly turns it :

> The rise of Adam's apple,
>   You fallen son of Eve,
> Enables you to grapple
>   With tones you can't conceive.

The merits of a word list with the Basic English aims are not from the nature of the case easy to assess. No mere glance over its columns will convey much even to those highly experienced in the work of writing and talking on widely varying topics in strictly limited vocabularies. There are not very many such persons as yet. The average teacher, however sound her methods, is not necessarily equipped to form an opinion. She may be skilled in keeping to a restricted word list while talking in class ; but talk suited to classes in elementary English keeps to narrow ground. It must. And the test of the Basic List concerns its general adequacy over the whole field of human affairs. The schoolroom is not the world. It is permissible to add a few nouns such as *desk* for schoolroom use (if the teacher cannot bring herself to class her desk as a table) without feeling that a world language need care for such a special need. Any *limited* list must be awkward at very many places—the other hundreds of thousands of words in English have their uses. It would be ludicrous to profess that any limited language can do all their work. And no informed person has ever made such a claim for Basic, though we suffer much from a type of critic who will suppose that it is made. Any user of Basic finds points at which for him it seems to stick ; he builds up a little list of words he wishes it contained ; he compares it with the lists of others and finds, as a rule, that they differ strangely ; the problem then becomes : has he discovered some defects in Basic or just some of his own verbal habits ?

Only the widest experience with Basic English can show what its adequacy is—within the bounds of its aims. I have tried to make its aims clear and draw their bounds. The experience with the language is now recorded in many books, some of which are listed in the Appendix. It should be added once again here that not every attempt to say something in Basic represents the best that Basic can do. There is bad Basic writing just as there is bad writing in any other English, as I have frequently reiterated. Allowing for this, however, it is abundantly evident that Basic can cover the field with an adequacy—in view of its limited resources—that would have been regarded as flatly impossible before Ogden's demonstration. Before 1927 no one had supposed that such a thing could be done, least of all some of those who, six years later, were bringing out rival word lists and " exposing " Basic, without ascertaining exactly what its principles or recommendations were.

Basic has naturally been subjected to a number of attacks. Few of them, I regret to say, have been from disinterested students. It is easy to present anything of which very little is known in a light that is disadvantageous. The remedy is not in controversy (which I have avoided here except for this mention) but in the growth of informed opinion.

These controversies did, of course, for a while make many teachers, administrators, and men of the world hesitate. Must there not be something queer if experts differ so violently ? There was something queer. Both the proposal and its technique were so novel that they upset deep-rooted assumptions and habits as well as powerful vested interests. The most violent of the attacks on Basic have been, it is true, withdrawn, as containing errors and misrepresentations. But attacks make more stir in the world than their withdrawal. Many hear of objections who never learn that they were not sustained. Such hostility, however, is perfectly normal. It is no more than an inevitable accompaniment to the appearance of something new in any old and established activity. The opposition of the canals to the railroads, and of the railroads in turn to the automobile, exemplified it. The degree of resistance has often been in fairly close relation to the value of the new technique. These things soon sink into oblivion. What remains is a new human possibility.

Chapter Four

AIMS AND POLICIES OF BASIC ENGLISH

STATEMENTS about the purposes of Basic English have from the first included two aims : the provision of a minimum secondary world language and the designing of an improved introductory course for foreign learners, leading into general English. And from the first it has been evident that these two aims appeal in different degrees to different sorts of people. It has also been evident that in some minds these two aims can get in one another's way and even cause confusions as to which features of Basic are most important for which aim. These confusions are understandable, although Ogden and other expositors of Basic have taken a good deal of care to make the distinction between the two aims clear. Nonetheless, misunderstanding continues. It is, in fact, at the root of most of the difficulty that many professional teachers of English experience in planning work with Basic English. It will therefore be worth while to attempt a fuller discussion of the two aims and of some of the points at which difference of aim should suggest a different emphasis and a somewhat different attitude toward the detail of the recommendations of Basic.

To take the supranational language aim first : a minimum world secondary language must put economy of vocabulary and syntax in a primary position. Next must come uniformity. The recommendations and provisions must be standardized and, for general guidance, fixed and strictly defined limits to the language must be laid down and insisted upon. The human being, fortunately for him, loves experiment and cherishes his freedom, but a main purpose of Basic English would be frustrated from the start if what was learned as Basic in different parts of the world did not tally. Furthermore, a certain regimentation is necessary if Basic English, merely as a proposal, is to preserve enough identity with itself to allow experiment and discussion to be profitable. If its various users were left free to diverge from its recommendations, making whatever innovations, extensions, or restrictions they pleased in the many directions that are possible, a time would soon come when no one could know what was being talked about under the heading " Basic English." Hence the copyrighting of the Basic List, and a certain firmness in rulings which have led to various misconceptions. An impression of pedantry and of a doctrinaire attitude quite naturally arises if the reasons for fixity and definiteness are not realized. Specifications for a universal minimum language must be precise and must be stable or we shall have nothing solid enough before us to be worth discussing. Fluidity would have been fatal.

The copyrighting of the Basic Word List, in particular, has been misinterpreted. It has been supposed to indicate a possessively defensive spirit. Early critics did not see that its purpose was, not to prevent the use of the system by capable people but to keep it intact for their use. Publications in Basic are, of course, in exactly the same position as regards copyright and permissions for reproduction as any other writings. The note at the foot of the Basic Word List points out that that page—the briefest specification of the system—has the same status. Obviously anyone is at liberty to write and talk in Basic. The protection afforded by copyright is only against commercial plagiarism and distortion. What had to be guarded against was a rapid and careless production of texts allegedly in Basic, but neither observing the principles nor using the teaching techniques made possible by the system. Such texts—of varying degrees of ineptitude—have nonetheless appeared, and if they have done nothing else they have shown the wisdom of exerting what measure of control is possible.

It was not easy to resist the temptation to let Basic be all things to all men. That was the easy line. Basic would have won innumerable adherents at once, but then the question would have been : " What are they adhering to ? " Ogden has not only been wise but he has been remarkably courageous in defining Basic so strictly. He has had to bear with many absurd charges—of premature canonization, of pontification, of arbitrariness ; he has had to endure much unimaginative opposition which a looser formulation could have easily enough removed. His reward has been that Basic English has remained a specific proposal, now demonstrated, tested, exemplified, and applied on a scale that would have been utterly impossible if he had yielded to the temptation to make its path into the world smooth by adroit compromise.

So much for the policy required for Basic as a minimum world secondary language. The policy appropriate to Basic as an introduction to general English has clearly to take into account other and somewhat more complex considerations. A self-contained language that shall be as compact, as easy, and as comprehensive as possible is one thing ; a set of first steps toward the language of Shakespeare and James Joyce is another. Furthermore, the inevitable professional outlooks of teachers of English, of school administrators, and of officials in ministries of education—all these come in to the picture.

More important still, if possible, are the very different circumstances under which English is taught. Sometimes, as in inland China, the teacher and the text must supply the only access to English the students have. No opportunities exist to learn anything but what is given to them in the classroom. But in other localities they are in close contact with all varieties of English. They see it on posters, meet it in newspapers, in conversation, on the radio. They pick up vocabulary, scraps of construction, idiomatic phrases, headline condensations—sometimes far in advance of anything a wise teacher would wish them to learn at that stage of their studies. The whole task of grading —of teaching one thing firmly before another is allowed to upset it—becomes an entirely different problem.

These things make the uses of Basic as an introduction to unlimited English far more variable and supple. For localities in which the students are all the while learning words and phrases that are not included in Basic, some of the recommendations that Basic stresses—as most desirable for students confined to a classroom and a text—lose their point. The advantages they offer will not be gained. But, even so, it is one thing to stumble upon complexities outside a classroom, and quite another to be introduced to them needlessly in the beginnings of instruction in the classroom. As there can be no guarantee that all pupils in an English-speaking locality will pick up the same advanced constructions, the plan for teaching within the framework will remain much the same. Precocious beginners in any language pick up idiomatic expressions beyond the level of their class. That does not mean that the class must stop and try to cope with them, any more than that we should deny the wider knowledge to the quicker student—if he has grasped the new expression so that he can use it correctly.

By far the most difficult situation arises, however, when teachers have to take over students with a considerable smattering of English that is broken English. They may be victims of a system of instruction that plunged them into too many and varied difficulties at a time, or they may be victims of circumstance, who have picked up what they could in the language without the help they needed. In either case, mending broken English by any method will be found to be much more difficult than making a clean start could ever be. Basic is no miracle worker here, but in the hands of an imaginative teacher it can be used to present a systematic review and a corrective in infinitely shorter time than most remedial treatment could. Drill in the fundamental sentence patterns of the language, with the Basic operators exercising common prepositions in their key senses, has saved many a student from despair over the English idiom. In such cases, of course, he is permitted the use of as many names of concrete objects outside the Basic List as he has picked up in his earlier study. These will be nothing more to him than problems in spelling and pronunciation. Their meaning is clearly demonstrable.

Broken English presents the most serious among more narrowly linguistic problems ; but infinitely more discouraging are the difficulties of the physically handicapped, which are now being re-examined in the light of what Basic teaching techniques have to offer. Take, for instance, the experiment now under way in England in the Margate Royal School for Deaf and Dumb Children, the largest institution of its kind in Europe. Here an average class of eight-year-olds and a backward class of fifteen-year-olds have both been working with Basic for about a year, and by the end of a second year may be ready to provide widely useful evidence of its effectiveness. Already the gain in both groups is striking, and both here and in schools for the blind where parallel experiments are in train, the value of a compact, nuclear vocabulary and a carefully graded set of syntax patterns cannot be overestimated. When the rate of learning is necessarily so slow, and the task of lip reading so heavy, students take kindly, indeed, to so easy a ladder to climb. The Margate School worked heretofore with a twelve-hundred-word vocabulary, which provides nothing comparable to the covering power of the Basic 850 ; and even so, few if any of its students get time to master in their school years the whole twelve hundred. With the Basic selection and revised methods they may well expect to cover the vocabulary in the junior school and exercise it in subject classes of wide variety during the remaining four years, which are at present handicapped by lack of language.

At the opposite end of the scale are mature students beginning

c

English, who, either alone or in small groups with a common language background, may acquire a grasp of the essentials of Basic from a concentrated attack upon *The ABC of Basic English* in their own languages first and later in English. *Basic Step by Step*, *Basic by Examples*, and others of the Psyche Miniature texts may then follow, in order to exercise the vocabulary on a varied and stimulating range of subjects. Serious English-speaking students of their own language will get from the *ABC* and *The Basic Words* not only a comprehensive picture of the Basic system but an insight into linguistic operations which they will find both interesting and useful.

It follows that a decision as to whether Basic, unmodified, is or is not the best introduction to general English cannot be made universally without close attention to the specific local conditions; nor can it be made without some close and realistic study of just how far in their English we expect our pupils to go, just what uses of their English we hope they will be able to make, and just what proportion of their precious time and energy they should invest in their study of English. We live in a world desperately in need of education. We have to ask ourselves very sternly of every school hour available whether it is being spent to the best individual and general advantage. Each of these hours has many claims on it. How can we see to it that as few hours as possible are wasted?

On the contribution that Basic may make here, two schools of thought have developed among those with actual field experience in teaching English in various parts of the world through Basic. There is room for them both, and in what follows I am not taking sides. It is unnecessary to do so, for in fact they need not conflict, though, through accidents of confusion, of divergent professional outlooks, of local differences in conditions, these two policies may sometimes seem to be opposed.

One school of thought regards Basic as primarily a minimum outfit of English, complete enough for its purposes in itself. That it is an excellent introduction to studies going further into English they agree. They have noted how careful Ogden was to make it such. But this is not, for them, its main function. They believe that most students of English (or any other language) do not, in fact, get very far, whether they study in class or by themselves. Even after years of work on current lines, most students, according to them, are still without enough mastery of the language to repay them for the energy and time they have invested. And this is due partly to poor methods of learning, but mainly to a mistaken goal. These students set for themselves, or are set by tradition, far too ambitious a programme : an attack, if not on the entire language, at least on such a variety of disconnected specimens and samples of it as to make failure inevitable. Their texts treat almost any word, any construction, any scrap or fragment of the language as though it were as worth while learning as any other. For example, the students are made to toil away at

> The sun rises in the east
> The sun sets in the west

before the senses of the verbs can possibly be clear to them. What wonder if (as I have heard in a class in China) those at the back of the room join in the chorus with " The sun *sits* in the west." *Rise* and *set* are no part of elementary English. *Come up* and *go down* are the proper business of a class at this stage ; the difficulties of *come* and *go* are quite enough for them, and no opportunity for developing these verbs should be lost for the sake of specific terms such as *rise* and *set* which the student may never have occasion to meet or use again. These scraps are mostly disconnected from one another ; or there is no time to point out the connections ; at worst the construction patterns they suggest conflict with one another. The outcome is confusion and frustration, a vain struggle which does very little either for the individual or for world communications. Defeat in any intellectual undertaking is bad for the learner. It is particularly bad in the learning of a language. Far better would it be if the student were to concentrate, instead, on acquiring a command of a properly organized minimum of the language, with which he could express himself over the widest possible field—adequately, if not eloquently—and become able to understand what is said to him or what he reads when expressed in a vocabulary and syntax not departing at too many points from the organized minimum or modicum he has learned. He will then have added verifiably and satisfyingly to his powers and can be in clear and useful communication with all who understand where the limits of his knowledge fall.

It will be admitted that this is an admirably realistic view. Few teachers will doubt that its assumptions as to the normal progress of average students in most school classes are correct. It is not difficult in almost any school in the hinterlands of China, India, or Africa to verify them. Unless special pressures, visits to English-speaking regions, or other advantages come to their aid, such students rarely gain any satisfactory command over any useful segment of the language. Although they have nominally learned some thousands of words instead of the Basic 850, any newspaper or novel sends them reaching for a bilingual dictionary—unless they are content, as they too often are, with no more than a hazy guess at the author's drift, which may settle into a habit difficult to cure—and even common constructions find them at a loss.

To the student of Basic, it is true, the newspaper presents still more new words. But he has his *General Basic Dictionary* (in which 20,000 non-Basic English words are defined in terms of his 850) to help him. And he has such a grasp of the English constructions (thanks to the intensive training he has undergone in handling a known and limited vocabulary with these very constructions) that his troubles are rarely with syntax. Why not then admit—so those of this view urge—that Basic is essentially a sufficient English for most learners' purposes ? Limit the task and make a good job of it. Supply more reading, news, radio talks, etc., in Basic or near it. Thereby we shall best attain the envisaged end of all this effort : real gain to the student and much needed improvement in world communications. It is true that these learners will not be admitted thus to the full understanding of English literature. But how many foreign students really get there anyhow ? And there are many ways in which Basic may be used as a key to even very difficult English writing.[1] To sum up : overambition and the pursuit of perfection are products of an academic vanity which forgets both what we are primarily aiming at and what is possible. By attempting too much we fail lamentably to teach even the little that school hours permit—those first steps without which the rest will never be gained. While granting—nay insisting—that Basic is no adequate substitute for a mastery of literary English, this school holds that a sound knowledge of it is a better and more attainable goal than a more impressive programme that leaves the student helpless in fact at all points.

[1]See Chapter Six where the use of Basic as an instrument of analysis and interpretation is considered.

I have stated this position at some length, partly because of its value as a challenge to academic attitudes, partly because it explains much in Ogden's policy, and in some of the opposition it has sometimes aroused, but chiefly in order to point out that those who dissent need not therefore reject Basic. For there is another school of thought, which equally believes in the utility of Basic while not agreeing wholly with the conclusions just outlined. For this school, the possibilities of Basic English as a world auxiliary language recede into the background. They are not necessarily denied but they are not taken as matters of such immediate practicability and importance. To realize them, according to this school of thought, action would have to be taken by governments, ministries of education, superintendents, headmasters' conferences, foreign language teachers' associations, and all manner of committees and advisory bodies of authorities and experts. And, on this view, experience shows that such bodies are by their very constitutions debarred in most instances from taking any such action as the adoption of some named and established system. To mention only one obvious factor, interests vested in other systems are involved, are indeed commonly represented on these bodies, and necessarily recommend compromise, further committees of experts, and the cultivation of " the open mind." Furthermore, these bodies are committed—by a defensive tradition than which nothing in the world is stronger, or in some ways more admirable—to the maintenance of academic standards. They are guardians of scholarship, in charge of examinations that must be at least as exacting and comprehensive as those of the rival body—and there always is one. Thirdly, these committees represent large bodies of teachers and understand well the problem of retraining that any considerable general change always entails. For these reasons, adoption of Basic as a general objective of instruction by governments or school systems is not, on this view, to be expected, however desirable it might be.

But if the prospects of Basic as a world auxiliary language are thus discounted by this school, they do believe in its immediate utility as a step toward a somewhat wider objective capable of being fitted without violent reorganization into existing syllabuses and schedules. And this, to them, is possible without any impairment of what they see as the characteristic virtues of Basic. They recommend that instruction in Basic proceed in the early stages exactly as on the other view. But at a point when some five hundred words had been acquired, together with all the chief constructions, there would be divergence. Those learning Basic as an international language complete in itself would go on to the rest of the Basic vocabulary without increase in variety of syntax. This would prepare them for reading texts in the sciences, abstracts of scientific papers, technical handbooks, general history, biology, economics, sociology, etc., written in Basic. Access to the thought of the world, so presented, would be opened to them without further years of struggle with the interminable complexities of the full language.

On the other hand, those using Basic as introduction to a wider English would begin to use words already learned as nouns from the Basic List in their verb forms (e.g., *he attempted* for *he made an attempt*) and make sundry other uses of Basic words beyond those recommended by the Basic system. Furthermore, a small number of strong verbs (*can*, for example, and *must*), unnecessary in Basic but of high frequency and therefore of much recognition value and very convenient, would be added.

The advantages claimed for this course by this school of thought are fourfold. (1) It allows the essential values of Basic procedure to be incorporated into schoolteaching with a minimum of disturbance to extant syllabuses and examinations, and thus allows a needed technical revolution in English teaching without exciting opposition or even remark. (2) It recognizes the fact that few learners of Basic having any contacts with English beyond the school walls fail to pick up additional words and constructions anyhow, often in distorted form. (3) It conciliates the teacher who finds it hard to go on postponing these expressions in her teaching. (4) It hastens somewhat the student's ability to read easy general English—and thus to tackle " unseen translations " in examinations. It does this without delaying his readiness to use the very valuable supplies of Basic reading matter, since *The General Basic Dictionary* includes definitions of the Basic words themselves. It is true that a student following this course will not, in a given time, gain an English with an active covering power equal to Basic. How short of this he remains at the end of the time will depend upon which and how many of the remaining 350 Basic words he postpones. But a compromise is possible there that would leave him not much behind the learner of strict Basic in this respect. In any case, this student who is planning a much more extensive study of

English should complete his knowledge of the Basic List at an early stage of his progress.

Such are the main positions of these two schools of thought. It will be seen that they differ, not in their estimate of the value of Ogden's simplification but in their choice of aim. For the first, Basic is a minimum world language beyond which students need not go except through the Basic dictionaries and into special fields—the Bible, science, economics, business. For the second, the aim is a wider knowledge of general English, toward which the essentials of Basic serve as a step. Both are agreed that there should be no extension of the verb list (or indeed of Column One of the Basic List) until the Basic operators are securely mastered, and this is in many ways the very heart of the Basic system.

Another glance over the Word List will make some of these points more concrete. Most words in Column One—the chassis —are very different from most of the words in the other columns. Without them the language does not work, will not go as a general system. The absence of particular words from the lists of nouns and adjectives would in many instances be merely so many local, specific inconveniences. Words in the two columns of " picturables " would be less hard to do without than most of those among the " general " four hundred. We could point or make a sketch as a way of eliciting the word we needed. The " general " words on the whole handle ideas, the " picturables " handle things. So the exact composition of the picturable list is less important from certain points of view than that of the general list. But in the very first steps of teaching English it is' clear that picturables and demonstrables have a special standing. We have to set out from them, if we are to make what our sentences mean, and how they mean it, visibly obvious to the learner. Thus sundry words, not of prime importance in the rest of the world's work, get included. *Chalk* is the representative example. We want, for teaching purposes, the names of things that will be lying about in the classroom, for the teacher to use in building up understanding of sentence forms.

Those of the second school of thought sometimes say, " Let the teacher add a few other names of things that are convenient for classroom purposes, if he pleases ! " There is no great objection, if only the names of visible, tangible things are intended. *Desk* would be an example. But with so many more important words waiting to be learned, it seems a pity to clutter up the as yet fragile structure in the pupil's mind with words of such limited use. The case is much stronger against such words as *class*, *period*, *assignment*, and other bits of pedagogic lingo which often creep in. These are words of quite other categories. They can be avoided without any trouble whatever. From the first a class can be handled without them and the precise jobs they perform can, at an early stage, be taken over by words and phrases that belong rightly to elementary English, the English the learner in any case needs and must certainly have if he is to go on further.

This is " talking shop," the peculiar problems of the language-teaching profession, and as such not the general reader's proper concern. " Shop," however, lets one in on the real problems of an undertaking as nothing else will. Persons other than Mark Twain most enjoy reading about things that are least their business. So the remainder of this chapter will deal with some of the questions the designer of a course in the teaching of Basic must settle.

The simplifications of Basic, by removing or postponing so much that has hitherto taken up the teacher's attention, have allowed a much more intensive study of the technique of grading than has ever before been possible with any language. The fewer the things you have to teach the more care you can give to the *order* in which you teach them. That order makes a world of difference to the learner's progress. Some things, when taught together, help one another. Some hinder one another. The ease of learning Basic as compared with a richer and more varied collection of words and constructions is not to be measured by the mere quantity of things to be learned. Much more important is the increased clarity and smoothness of exposition which the Basic economies make possible.[2] This is an aspect of Basic which has not hitherto been much presented in writings on the subject, and has therefore not come to the attention of any but experts. But it is a large part of the grounds for the claims of Basic.

One obvious problem is a decision about *will* and *shall*. The author once wandered into a classroom up in the big bight of the Yangtze in upper Yünnan. The blackboard was covered with a complex and meticulous analysis of the uses of these two words. Here at last, he thought, I shall meet a teacher of English who

[2] See the Teachers' Edition of *Learning the English Language*, Books I, II, III, Houghton Mifflin Co., 1942-43.

can talk it. The hope was vain. In the ensuing conversation neither of us said in English anything that was understood by the other. The analysis hung there all the time, mocking our endeavours.

In thousands of classrooms all over the world similar things are frustrating the efforts of students to learn English. The right decision is to banish *shall* altogether from elementary English. Pedantry, the price that many fine minds have to pay for their accomplishment, may make some persons wince at the thought of " Will I ? " Yet the facts of the geographical and *social* distribution of " Will I ? " and " Shall I ? " are conclusively in favour of postponing *shall*. The right time for the learner to tackle the *shall-will* entanglement comes when he has learned nearly everything else in the language. He won't have used " Will I ? " often enough to have formed a fixed habit. We use it, most of us, somewhat rarely. And if he did, the worst inference anyone could draw would be that he had had a Scottish-American scholar as a teacher ! As Jespersen remarks, " The Scotch and Irish, hence also the Scotch-Irish parts of America, use constantly *I* (*we*) *will* :

> We'll have rain before the week is out.
> I am not going to live to be an old man. I will not get old.

They even use *will* in questions like :

> O, when will I forget that ? (Scott)
> What time'll I come for you ? (' am I to ')
> What will I say when they ask me ? "[3]

Those who know most about the history and actualities of English will be least likely to wish *shall* upon a first-year course. Here is Logan Pearsall Smith upon it : " One of the most elaborate and wonderful achievements of the Genius of the Language in modern times is the differentiation of the uses of *shall* and *will*, a distinction not observed by earlier writers, and so complicated that it can hardly be mastered by those born in parts of the British Islands in which it has not yet been established."[4]

What does this comparatively new and surprisingly subtle

[3] *Essentials of English Grammar*, p. 275.
[4] *The English Language*, p. 29.

C*

distinction do for us ? It plays with nuances on the borderland
between predicting the future and asserting volition. Thus it is
in talking about oneself that subtleties chiefly arise. Jespersen
puts it as follows : " In the first person *will* does not lend itself
so well as in the others to the expression of mere futurity, as *I
will* and *we will* are so extensively and so naturally put in requisi-
tion to express volition, and as the other auxiliary, *shall*, has come
to be much used with *I* and *we* to express mere futurity. Still *I
(we) will* is gaining ground in this function where strict grammarians prefer *shall*, and this cannot be thought unnatural,
seeing that there are many border cases in which it is difficult
to know whether volition or pure future is meant, and that the
abbreviated form *'ll* is so handy."[5] It is always hard to see where
prophecies about one's doings end and mere intentions and
hopes must take their places. *Shall* and *will* drag us into that
cloudy realm beloved of Milton's demons, who

> reason'd high
> Of Providence, Foreknowledge, Will and Fate,
> Fixt Fate, free will, foreknowledge absolute,
> And found no end in wandring mazes lost.

Hard-and-fast rulings here belong to a pre-Freudian linguistics
that had not heard of unconscious wishes. In talking about our
own future we do not know how far we are interfering with it.
And if we do not know, no grammarian shall (will) tell us !

Across this debatable ground comes, with *shall*, the equally
doubtful implication of obligation, clearer and stronger with the
form *should* (ought to). But even *should* so often suggests only
probability—" He should be here soon. He left in good time "—
that clearness is not enhanced by too early an appearance of
should in a learner's vocabulary. The outcome of such reflections
—which might be continued to great length—is that Basic is
wise in postponing *shall* and in limiting *will*, in the earlier stages,
to the simple neutral indication of the future. Distinctions
between the two are no matters for beginners in the language.[6]

[5] Jespersen, *op. cit.*, p. 274.

[6] The opinion of that strong supporter of Basic, the late Sterling Andrus
Leonard, may be quoted : " John Fell, in his *Essay towards an English
Grammar*, 1784, apparently came closer than anybody in either the
eighteenth or nineteenth centuries to describing the true status of *shall*
and *will* : ' *Will*, as an auxiliary term, is a mere sign of futurity, set
before the infinitive mode . . . *shall*, even as an auxiliary sign, always

Meanwhile, Basic of course has many clearer ways of expressing the various implications carried by *shall* and *should*.

Most of our problems, however, are not solved so simply—by excluding or postponing a source of unnecessary difficulty. They concern the order in which two equally necessary forms should be learned. A very elementary example is : Which should come first : *I gave it to him*, or *I gave him it ?* Here parallels with *I got it from him*, *I took it from him*, *I put it on the table* lead us at once to postpone *I gave him it* until there is no longer any risk of its upsetting the general pattern. This is usually the ruling consideration. How can we best keep patterns that are just forming in the learner's mind from unnecessary disturbance ? Once they are securely established, the rival will no longer be a danger.

A more complex example comes with *I give it* and *I am giving it*. Few native speakers of English who do not have to teach it realize how tricky our uses of the expanded and the unexpanded tenses are, especially the present tense. We say (i.e., as a rule we do) *I give*, *I take*, etc., when we mean we habitually do. We ordinarily say *I am giving*, *I am taking*, etc., when we mean we propose to or probably will do so. We rarely mean with either form that we are actually now, at this very moment, performing the action. This is unreasonable of us. The words logically should mean that. But, in fact, we seldom have occasion to describe what we are actually doing. The people we are talking to can see that for themselves ! So more recondite meanings have taken over the present for their purposes.

One of the worst hardships, among many that afflict a teacher of beginner's English, is that she is forced to be perpetually talking for her students about what she is actually doing. Though in general the future and the past are of far more use to us than the present tense used of present time, they cannot be understood by beginners except with reference to the present which divides them. So we do well to use the present tense for that—as an introduction to them—and then drop it until the students are ready to take up the more recondite uses of the present tenses

denotes something more than mere futurity, and constantly implies either obligation, possibility, contingency, or something conditional, and very often several of these together.' " See *The Doctrine of Correctness in English Usage*, 1700-1800, p. 74. Those wishing to pursue the matter further will do well to read Jespersen's able summary in *Essentials of English Grammar*, pp. 279-81.

instanced above. Even so, we have still the problem : Should we use *I give* or *I am giving*, etc., for this purpose ?

There is much to be said on both sides. Considerations of the learner's mother tongue are relevant when we know what it is. But in civic education classes in Massachusetts, for example, there may be as many as ten mother tongues in the room. The order in which we are going to introduce our verbs is relevant, too—especially as regards the interrogative (and a great debate can rage over how soon that should come). For example, we ask, " Do you see him now ? " not " Are you seeing him now ? " —unless we want to make one or another of two very different inquiries (" Are you habitually meeting him ? " or " Will you be meeting him ? "). But we do ask, " Are you saying ' pin ' or ' pen ' ? " not " Do you say ' pin ' or ' pen ' ? "—unless again we have a curiosity of wider scale. We answer the question about what is actually happening with, " I see him " not with " I am seeing him," and with " I am saying " not with " I say." These two verbs, in fact, reverse one another's practice here.

There are various equally good solutions of the *I give-I am giving* problem—equally good if we keep to any one of them. The uneconomic thing is to mix them, for thereby we unnecessarily mix up the learner's wits.

These will probably be samples enough of the troubles of a grader. The grader we meet on the highway works through treating the road with a lordly sort of indiscrimination. The text writer has to be as discriminating as he can, put himself in the learner's place, and yet take as long a view of all he is going to meet as possible. Only so can he make the path of learning smooth.

It will be evident from these examples that the task of organizing the presentation of the first five hundred or so words of English, in the fashion that will make them and their ways most fully comprehensible to the learner, is considerable. As we have already remarked, it can now, thanks to the analyses and economies of Basic, be carried further than had previously been supposed. Grading is no matter of assigning equal numbers of new words and new constructions to each lesson. It is a matter of entering as fully and imaginatively as we can into the learner's actual processes and arranging things so as to give him as lucid and as reasonable a task as possible. Teachers in general have been far too ready to say that one point in English is harder than another without entering into the all-important questions :

" How has either point been prepared for, and how could it be prepared for ? " There is no such thing as " difficulty " in the abstract. How difficult any step is depends upon what has led up to it and how the learner has been prepared. That is a fundamental principle in any sound theory of learning. To suppose otherwise and forget the relevance of conditions is as if physicists should confuse *mass* with *weight*. The comparable error is as inexcusable in a language teacher.

This developed conception of grading, it may be noticed, is an extension, into language teaching, of a principle that has everywhere been gaining ground in educational theory and practice : respect the mind of the learner. Let him see whenever possible the why and how of what he is asked to do. Give him an intelligible structure to study. Don't just shovel so much miscellaneous, unrelated information daily on to his plate !

On the whole those teachers who have studied Basic have been very eager to co-operate in this more arduous examination of the problems of grading. And there is good hope that in time a recognition of the real complexity of their work, and the degree of skill and technical training required to do it well, will effect a much needed raising of the status of this branch of the teaching profession. At present, language teachers are a depressed class—underprivileged economically and undervalued in public esteem. There is a general impression that almost anyone who knows English is fitted to teach it. From this the best teachers suffer acutely and most unjustly. It would be interesting to see how many university professors of literature, for example, were they set to teaching beginners' English, could equal them in actual *teaching*, as opposed to display of accomplishment or erudition.

But there remains one widespread misconception, with roots deep in human stupidity, if not in worse things, which must be removed before any such improvement in the language teachers' status, or much improvement in methods of instruction, can occur : the half-conscious identification of the language learner with the young child. This crops up as an obstruction everywhere, sometimes in such unlikely quarters that perhaps a few strong phrases here in closing this chapter may be of use.

A leading educator, for example, will question the validity of grading, on the ground that it departs from " the natural way in which we all learn our native language." Or a teacher, glancing over a text, will remark, " These seem very advanced words." *Puppy* and *puss* are more the sort of thing he is accustomed to in first-year courses, which are, in fact, still widely under the sway of the muddled idea that a beginner in a language must be a beginner in life. Interests supposedly juvenile spread sticky paws all over them. This preconception is astonishingly strong. It is a *pre*conception because it could hardly be the product of thought. Even a twelve-year-old taking up the study (in his school text) of a foreign language is very far removed from the infant babbling his way into his native tongue. There is no *reason* why language texts should have toadied to the supposed tastes of this infant. But in obvious and in disguised ways he remains still one of the major enemies of all language teaching everywhere.

As being allegedly unable to think, this infant—and all learners with him—is to be given his proper mental food, language, as he receives it while crawling the floors of a garrulous household, language at random, unarranged, with all the lawlessness of its multifarious impacts unmitigated. Look ! says this party. How miraculously the infant acquires and puts forth words. This is Nature's doing. Can you with all your cunning grading do as well ? Leave things to Nature. Follow wise Nature. She knows best.

Idle to reply that the maturer mind, when it puts anything like the time into learning a language that the child does, and allows as little to distract, will beat the child hollow in everything, except the perfection of his accent. Idle to remark that a method adapted to twelve hours a day will not serve for five separated hours a week, or to point out that in no other subject do we just leave the learner in an unarranged environment. Why not leave the learning of arithmetic to Nature ? Idle to observe that most activities that make us human are departures from wise Nature's ways. Idle, in fact, to dispute at all, unless we see that there is a hidden politic behind these views. These students of language are not being consigned to Nature for their own good. Behind the whole position is an obscure but powerful, secret but undeniable, retired but interfering feeling that it is a bad thing to encourage anyone to use his brains on deeper things than anecdote swapping, detective fiction, and mechanical design. Least and last of all should he use it on language. It is easy to think that word magic—the fear and faith which protect language from free inspection—is the laughable or deplorable affliction of a few spellbinders (and the spellbound) or that it is the quaint invention of some cranks. But the cult has had its haunts in less conspicuous quarters than Nuremberg and The Palazzo di Venezia. Having survived in the measure in which it was subtle, its sanctuary is too often the schoolroom.

Chapter Five

BASIC ENGLISH TEACHING FILMS

LEARNING a language is a little like filling a tub that leaks. If you do not fill it faster than it leaks, despair is the only outcome. By trying to fill it *too* fast you may increase the leakage, but most minds, like tubs, slowly close their cracks if kept continuously moist. The oozing ceases. Most of the secrets of efficient learning concern the causes of forgetting.

Anyone who has read Ogden's *ABC of Psychology* (in America called *The Meaning of Psychology*), or looked through the volumes of *Psyche* (the journal of psychology he founded and edits) will not be surprised to hear that the problems of forgetting and remembering had a large part in the design of Basic. This design helps the learner in four ways :

1. By cutting down what has to be remembered to a minimum.

2. By arranging automatically for the most frequent repetition (in slightly changed settings) of the most important items, the minimum apparatus of structure words.

3. By giving the material presented the highest degree of intelligible interconnection and by replacing memorization wherever possible, by insight and understanding. Too many language courses in the past have offered words to the learners as though they were nonsense syllables, or put mere drill in the place of comprehension.

4. By the use of visual material on the largest scale. The Basic operators (*give, get, put, take*) and the directives (*see* diagram p. 31) that are the pivots and pins of the whole machine are visualizable in their key senses in the fullest measure, and these senses may be illustrated for the eye in countless ways. Their extensions and dependent senses are linked with them by visual metaphor.

It is a commonplace of pedagogy that what is learned through the most senses together will be most readily retained, and in assembling a collection of words (and a system of meanings for them) to serve as a minimum language this should on no account be overlooked. The eye and the visual imagination behind it are indeed invaluable adjuncts and allies to the ear in language learning. They can and do aid the ear even in its organization of the auditory part of the work ; written words can help us to hear them. But in the organization of meaning, the eye, if given its chance, easily leads. It is the most comprehensive, the most intelligent, the most interconnective, the subtlest, the supplest, the most discriminative, and the most docile of our organs. The more work we can hand over to the reflective and understanding eye the better will the whole work be done and the more clearly will it be remembered.

The eye supplies the chief framework within which most meanings may best be arranged and through which they may be linked with one another in the most ways. It is the eye and the ideas of space and of space relations, over which sight rules, that do most to bring the various deliveries of our other senses into connection with one another. Our thoughts, we say, " take shape." The intelligible world is normally visual through and through ; the physical world is a world of space ; the other worlds (even the world of time) are largely ordered for us by space metaphors. We can hardly talk of what is *in* our minds without using spatial terms. Our language bears witness at every turn to the fact that we learn most easily by seeing—optically or with the mind's eye in imagination.

We understand, for example, by *seeing the point*. Things become *clear* to us, *lucid, perspicuous, transparent, evident*—they *shine* in upon and *illuminate* our minds, *brighten* our darkness, *reveal* themselves to us, and the rest. The prevalence of these metaphors of light and vision in our ways of talking about how we learn is highly significant. It shows how important visual understanding is as a guide in ordering other understandings. When we locate a sound, we do so through a reflex that switches the eyes in the direction of the source of the sound, a reflex depending upon the difference of phase of the sound wave in our ears. This fact might serve as a symbol of the predominance of vision, actual or imaginary, in interpreting all our perceptions, sensory or intellectual.

It follows that the proportion of the meanings of a language that can be visually presented is an enormously important factor in determining the ease with which it can be learned and retained. Ogden from the outset was careful to develop this aspect of Basic to the utmost degree compatible with its other aims. We have seen how the key senses of the operators may be presented in visible acts. We can actually see what *give* and *get, put* and *take, keep* and *let, go* and *come, have* and *make, say, see* and *send* mean in their simplest physical senses. Similarly we can see what the directives (*in*, *on*, and the rest) mean. The same is true of as many as possible of the other words on the Basic List. The separation of the two hundred " picturables " on the Basic List is a witness to this preoccupation. But this separation does not imply that the meanings of the other words are not able to be illustrated and explained pictorially. A surprising number of them are, and Ogden in fact has, from the first, had in progress a pictorial guide to the Basic words, presenting their root senses, expansions, and specializations systematically. When it is finished this will be a new type of teaching aid—an " eye opener " as to the possibilities of vision in language teaching (see meanwhile, *Basic Picture Talks* by L. W. Lockhart, 1942).

It is inevitable that at this point the greatest of the new modern instruments of education should present itself for consideration. The sound motion picture, almost unused as yet for such purposes, with television on its heels, is the proper channel for language teaching in the near future, as certainly as Basic English, for the reasons I have been outlining, is the uniquely prepared material with which to demonstrate its powers. Early overenthusiastic estimations of the powers of the cinema in teaching make it desirable, however, to go into the grounds for this view with some care.

It has been known for some years that standard teaching in a number of subjects based on standard texts, gains strikingly in effectiveness if accompanied by sound motion films presenting some part of the same material. Perhaps the most authoritative research on this point yet published is that of Dr. Philip Justin Rulon.[1]

Using a specially designed film and a specially written text, and checking the results with very carefully balanced control classes, he found that in teaching physiography, for example, the immediate student achievement, when films were used, was 20.5 per cent better than without them. More significant still, the retained gain (after three and a half months) was 38.5 per cent greater. Most significant of all, *for items common to the film and to the classroom presentation*, the film group was more than 55 per cent superior to the control group in retained learning. Such results are supported by many other investigations. It is worth adding that the evidence from such inquiries is not favourable

[1] *The Sound Motion Picture in Science Teaching*, Harvard Studies in Education, Vol. XX, Harvard University Press, 1933, pp. 98-104.

to films that merely present a teacher in action. Only when the picture is so designed as to make its own independent visual presentation of the meanings are such results to be expected ; that is, here, only when the English taught is Basic.

This evidence, striking enough in connection with such subjects as physiography, suggests far more impressive possibilities in teaching Basic. For whereas in these physiography films only a proportion of the items were common to the film and the classroom instruction, in teaching Basic every word, phrase, and construction can be jointly presented by the teacher and the film. We can, therefore, expect the retention of this whole sequence of linguistic facts to be increased over half as much again. Every teacher, and most of us who have attempted to learn any foreign language, can realize the implications here. With any well-designed sequence of lessons, we are continuously building, or attempting to build, new accomplishments upon foundations supposedly learned. The whole trouble is that these supposed foundations will, for most of us, deliquesce like quicksand. Our new constructions founder because what we thought we knew a week ago will not stay put. That is our trouble in language learning. The new is the enemy of the old, if the old is not solid enough to bear up under the superstructure. A 50 per cent increase in stability means certain victory at innumerable points. It gives us the time needed to confirm our earlier acquisitions by new exercise ; and the time factor here is decisive.

There are other reasons, no less strong, for believing that a sound-motion-picture programme for Basic can teach enough English for general purposes in a period which would seem fantastically short to teachers accustomed to the usual rate of progress. An obvious reason concerns the intensity of study that such films permit. There is a limit to the number of times we can go through the same lesson with a teacher. There is no such limit to the number of times we can submit ourselves to the running of a film. With suitable pauses of undistracted vacancy (this may well be important, for there is some evidence that other interests and activities following immediately on a period of study can play Old Nick with what was learned) we can take our lesson from the film again and again, until it is, as it were, rammed home into our nervous systems as by a rivet gun. (The key patterns can be put on film-loops and repeated so many times a minute, if required, very much as on this analogy.)

Another reason concerns the quality of attention that motion

pictures command as compared with other ways of presenting a
subject matter. Most lecturers who have used motion pictures in
connection with talks will agree that their audiences find it
easier to attend to the pictures and that they give a more continuous, more undivided and receptive attention thereto. Why
this is so is not at present clear. It has been suggested that one
cause is a firm, general conviction that pictures are *entertainment*,
coupled and contrasting with an equally firm general conviction
that lectures are *instruction*. There is an age-old war in our
tradition between the two. " Poets," said Horace, " wish to
delight or to instruct or to combine the two." Educational
films, for our contemporary culture, combine the two in a
miraculous fashion. Two impulses in the soul, one that seeks
amusement, the other that seeks improvement, find in the
teaching picture an unexpected joint satisfaction, and we go all
out for it. However this may be and whatever the reasons,
experience with war-industry instructional films seems to clinch
the fact that more can be taught quicker by talking pictures
than by any of the older conventional methods.

More specifically, the peculiar need in language teaching for
multiple repetition with slight variations points to the films.
Many classes learn to understand their teacher well enough,
but they are baffled by the first speaker with a different accent,
pitch, and rhythm. In films we can vary the speaking voices
indefinitely and by contrasts of voices weave in the repetitions
we need without wearying the audience. Similarly, the cinema
resources can display the range of a word's senses in manifold
examples as no textbook or teacher possibly could. Again, we
can vary the *order* in which sentences and their meanings are
presented—sometimes letting the words come first, to be followed
by the picture-borne meaning, sometimes giving the meaning
first and setting the finding of the right words as a problem to
the audience, which the following sentence will correct. A good
teacher can do this, of course, in her classroom, within the limits
of her available equipment, but the variety of arrangements
possible to the film is greater. And since a good teacher is an
unusual teacher, good films can lead, by example, to improvement in technique in the classroom. Films, I may add, do not get
tired. The best teacher at the end of a day loses some of her force.

It is sometimes supposed that cinema audiences must necessarily be passive. This is simply a mistake. There is in practice
no difficulty at all in getting a very high degree of audience

participation. When the purpose of a film and the needs of the audience require it, a film can easily be designed to make an audience talk back at it to any degree desired. Learners who have their motives for participating will quite spontaneously fill in prepared pauses with the appropriate sentences from the second showing onward. I have watched classes of grandmothers and their grandchildren joining in so—without any previous direction. Some confident soul starts, others pick it up and so the chorus grows. This happens even with a very rough test reel by no means adjusted to secure a maximum hold on its audience.

The test reel in question was the outcome of a spell of work at the Walt Disney Studio made possible for me by the Rockefeller Foundation. Though by no means a finished product, it was enough to show that there are no technical obstacles in the way of presenting a language through films—from the very first steps to the highest flights desired—provided only that the material has been visually organized through and through. It seems likely that a full course in Basic should use some thirty short reels, of less than ten minutes each, though just what rate of progression in the content of the reels would be most effective is a problem for further study. All the essential constructions of English and some five hundred Basic words can be presented without congestion in about twenty such reels, and the sequences can be made entirely self-explanatory without any use of any other language. The actions in the pictures take the place of references to any mother tongue. This on general pedagogic grounds is very desirable. Practically it means that such a film course would be equally of service to schools and learning groups in every part of the world.

To *literate* groups, that is. The qualification will seem very important, if we bear in mind that something like two thirds of the inhabitants of the planet are either unable to read at all or unable to read in our alphabet. If we are to have a common second language for the world we must clearly make a literacy campaign part of our programme. There is no doubt whatever that to teach Basic or any other language efficiently we must use written words in our instruction, and, after all, ability to read and write in the language is a main part of the aim. It is possible to design a Basic teaching film course that would omit writing and address itself merely through pictures and sounds to illiterates ; but such a course would be heavily handicapped. The script that should accompany the spoken sentences (as sub- or super-titles) is of immense service in displaying the structure of the language. Grammar takes its name from writing, and without this aid to the eye in analysing sentence forms progress is necessarily slow, as illiterates' classes in the U.S.A. show. The teaching of reading and writing is therefore an essential part of the programme for illiterates.

Illiterates in the U.S.A. are most of them over forty-five, especially among the foreign born. The Alien Registration Programme has found approximately seven hundred thousand illiterates among its charges. It uses a rather strict definition of illiteracy (inability to sign one's name after some fashion). With a much wider definition, the Selective Service System found itself rejecting a quarter of a million otherwise fully eligible young men in the first year of its operation. Illiteracy, therefore, is not a remote problem affecting only the conjectural future of people in Africa, South America, India, and China. It is also a United States problem, of no mean dimensions. New resources and techniques for dealing with it concern every government and every educational authority in the world. Even those countries that enjoy the highest literacy rates[2] need to study every means of smoothing the path into reading and writing, and no educator will have to be reminded of the collateral problems that beset the retarded reader, or of the millions all over the world who, largely through these difficulties, leave school without attaining fourth-grade standards. It is worth considering, therefore, what Basic on the one hand and motion-picture teaching on the other, and the two conjointly, can do to improve the situation.

Basic as a teaching technique is essentially a reaction against trying to tackle everything at once. It has sorted out the words that will do most and graded their introduction so as to enable the learner to *see* (in every sense of *see*) what the words do. Its principle is the postponement of what is as yet unnecessary and only distracting. Let each successive problem be freed, so far as possible, from rival problems that will disturb its due understanding and solution. The relevance of the four main features of the Basic teaching design—economy, repetition, intelligibility, and visual support—to the early stages of reading will be evident.

[2]According to its official figures, Japan occupies a proud eminence here : its literacy rate is 100 per cent ; on which figure and how it was arrived at we may each form our own opinion.

In fact a text[3] written in the first place as an introduction to Basic for literate aliens in Massachusetts, has been found of singular service for retarded readers whose native tongue is English. But it is possible to carry the same principles down to the very first introduction to written words and letters. By doing so we can contrive a great simplification of the tasks we set the beginning reader.[4] We can thus take the learner at the earliest moment to a text where he will meet the words and sentence structures we have taught him to read, at work with a few other words over a wide range of subject matter. The covering power of Basic is very helpful here. The student then is no longer learning to read : he is already free to use his reading power on matter interesting to him. With this encouragement he can go out into other material to any extent which his oral knowledge of English permits. Closely interwoven with this course in reading should be a parallel course in writing. The exercise of making the letters and words is, of course, of the greatest help in recognizing them. The two activities go naturally together. In both, I believe the teaching film can and should play a large part.

One of the prime *difficulties of beginning reading is the control of the point of maximum attention. The film can surpass the teacher here. It can show the letters being formed and taking their places, the words taking their places in sentences, and what the sentences say—all with a calculated timing and a minimum of distraction unattainable by other means. So, too, with the motions of writing. Writing is a minute form of dancing. The simplifications possible in a properly graded course can be best reproduced and preserved by films worked over with this in view. Only the best teachers at their best moments are likely to match them in lucidity. And there are all too few such teachers available. Illiteracy films, reinforcing the spoken word with a graded introduction to written symbols, and employing every sort of pictorial and kinesthetic aid to learning at each step, are what is needed. For wide regions of the world they are a necessary introduction to films teaching Basic.

It is wiser at present not to attempt estimates as to the time

---

[3] *Learning the English Language : A Book for the Men and Women of All Countries*, Houghton Mifflin Co., 1942.

[4] Materials illustrating these principles of grading in the teaching of reading to beginners have been prepared by the Harvard Commission on English Language Studies.

required to teach Basic through sound motion pictures. The data are not yet available. Not enough is known about a number of relevant factors to make guessing profitable at present. For example, after how many viewings does a *language* film, which does not use language to present something else but uses other things to present language, cease to instruct ? When, in short, does the learner get through with it and need the next, more advanced film ?   Naturally films lend themselves especially well to purposes of review.

My experience suggests that with the elements of Basic—the first steps where all is new—the learner can go on noting new things about the sounds, the syntax, the implications, through a great number of showings. My reference earlier in this chapter to the rivet gun might mislead. Isolable phonetic, semantic, and grammatical points can be hammered home ; but the general attitude taken up in watching a language film is not that of the board into which nails are being driven. It is an attitude of alert exploration and eager anticipation full of the drama of success and failure, corroboration and correction. That is the surface play of the intelligence. Meanwhile, in the lower levels, stable sequences—word order, inflection, patterns, and the rest—are being grafted in to the memory.

After a number of viewings, varying with the individuals, a learner comes to be able to recite stretches of the script. This is something and may be much—if these stretches contain the main patterns of English, and so give him his model sentences, his pronoun system, and so on. Many teachers have found that memorized passages are highly valuable to the student. But such memorizing is, of course, a minor aim, a by-product that may yet be a step to something higher. The something higher is understanding of how the English words and sentence forms work, the understanding that enables one to take them and say new things with them. I stress this because it might be thought that language films would be unable to develop such understanding and could only serve as packers of the memory. But to think so is to underestimate the technical resources and range of the powers of the sound-motion-picture medium. It is at least as good at provoking thought as at imparting fact, though as yet both these uses have remained relatively undeveloped.

Meanwhile, it is incontestable that the cinema is the chief agency we possess that tends inherently of its own very nature toward world unification or, at least, world uniformity.   The pictures are a world language already. This visual language has many dialects, but most of them are mutually comprehensible. By and large, pictures are universal. Or a little experience with them makes them so. Peoples in the remotest corners of the earth and living in cultures least akin to ours learn our pictorial dialects with surprising ease and become thereby accessible, in a disconcerting degree, to what we find to say with our pictures. So far those who have most reflected upon this great new power that is now loose in the world (and that still mightier power-to-be, television, the offspring of the cinema and the radio) have on the whole been frightened by the possibilities presented. I need not expatiate on the dreadful visions of an entire world degraded to joint enjoyment of the lowest levels of commercial diversion or distraction which have been conjured up. These warnings were needed, no doubt. But in an age intent on reconstruction and aware of the necessity of using in that work every power we possess or can develop, it is more important still to insist upon the unparalleled opportunities for the sane service of mankind that the cinema offers.

A common world pictorial language ready to hand, and already at work, is the appointed vehicle for teaching its common verbal language to the world. Through and in conjunction with that common language it is the natural, the technically proper means of teaching what is necessary if the world is to enjoy any unity of purpose and hence any peace. A world inevitably made one through its physical communications will destroy itself unless it can be united also through intellectual and moral communications. When ideas can get everywhere in a flash, it becomes really necessary to see that the best ideas get priority of transport. The cinema, as recent applications have brought out, could in skilled hands teach anything—from the details of engineering practice to the postulates of democracy. The sciences and the arts alike are within its scope—though, of course, adequate ways have still to be worked out of presenting arithmetic, algebra, geometry, mechanics, chemistry, and the rest ; or design, composition, harmony, colour relations, and the techniques of the other arts : or logic, literary criticism, psychology, and elementary philosophy. To discover through experiment how all this may best be done will be the task of generations of teachers. That it can be done and that it can bring new orders of general human welfare within our reach is now certain. We are not yet in sight of the limitations of the film as an instrument of education.

Those who would attempt to limit it now have not sufficiently explored its capabilities in new design and new devices. All that man has done in the past in the routine of teaching, and much that has been physically impossible to him, is within its potential range. We should not let ourselves be too much influenced by the fact that it has been hitherto, on the whole, a toy. That very fact, by associating pictures so firmly with pleasure has prepared the way for its greater uses. The cinema has grown up, at last, through instructional films made to meet war needs. We have to turn it now to the service of reconstruction and peace.

Chapter Six

BASIC ENGLISH FOR READING BETTER

As I write, the college world is concerned over the manifest ignorance of its students of American history as revealed by a test published in the New York *Times*. History teachers are under attack. More and better history courses—that seems to be the popular remedy. From time to time for one subject or another these disturbances of the general equanimity occur. More and better courses are as a rule the prescription. But amid the confusion the voice of the experienced teacher can usually be heard saying : " Didn't you know ? Why be so surprised ? What will more courses or better books do for students who can't understand them ? It is the same in all subjects. All subjects need ability to read ; ability to make out what is being said ; nothing very recondite, only the sheer plain sense of a simple statement. Our students haven't got that. They can't read, or listen. Better do something about *that* instead of pressing overworked professors for more and better courses at the wrong end of the line for students who aren't prepared to take them in."

If we consult this uncomfortable critic further he will take us to the shelves where the school English texts stand row upon row, series after series. They are things that all students of our culture should frequently take in their hands. Historians will. There is very little to choose among most of them; they are made to standard, are minor variations on an established pattern. They propose to show that reading is fun, that listening is interesting, that language is really a human possession and its use something that every child will enjoy. These are their chosen themes. Accordingly, assorted youngsters are gathered together in their pages (with the aid of pictures) to hear discourse upon them. How to be popular through your use of language is a favourite opening gambit. How to be a welcome member of the group. How to bring out the awkward ones. How to keep the conversation up. How to give everyone a chance to talk. How to raise topics on which everyone will have something to say (pets, games, hobbies). How to chime in when your turn opens with the right anecdote which everyone will want to hear. Those anecdotes ! By the time they come, the text writers have got into their stride. One pointless, improbable pet after another is trotted out to perform at the supposedly right juvenile level. All this with a view to a re-enactment of the horrible business. It has been fun to read about this group. Now it will be fun to be the group, and do the talking with our own anecdotes, won't it ? So the text suggests. The poor children then nominally listen to one another, while thinking out their own " contributions."

Such are the beginnings, and the proverb will remind us that first steps count most. No one will doubt that children who get little guidance in conversational behaviour at home must be given it in school ; nor will anyone deny that the material used must be suited to their interests. It is the conception of those interests that is at fault, in its underestimation of their capacity to be concerned with more profitable matters. There is nothing in these anecdotes to arouse thought, nothing for the mind to exercise or develop its powers upon, nothing to be understood except in the most superficial fashion. And later, when the text writer does attempt to put some meat into his paragraphs, the minds he is training are, not surprisingly, unprepared to assimilate it. What wonder if they give it only that degree of attention which they are accustomed to find appropriate and sufficient ! What wonder if the required sort of interest is then lacking ! It is not the immaturity of children's minds that should be blamed, but their lack of exercise.[1]

This is a composite portrait of many such reading books. It must not be taken as representing any one rather than any others of the type. They differ in detail, but they are as alike as men's suits, and their uniformity has much the same origin. Together they represent the collective wisdom of the teaching profession as at present advised. My reader will therefore realize, I hope, that I am attacking something in these paragraphs. These books are what the teachers of English believe in and ask for. It is not the wicked publishers who force bad books (for vast sales) on helpless teachers. Dorothy Thompson was wrong. It is the teachers who like such books and will have no others. They have, of course, to be brought up to date frequently but, as with fashions, that consists in making such changes as will keep them the same.

Meanwhile, higher up the education ladder (but a ladder is too strenuous an image here ; I should say " lower down the assembly

[1] I present these views at length in *Interpretation in Teaching*, especially in the Introduction.

line ") the bitter cries go up : " Students cannot read ! They do not understand what is said to them—whenever it steps up from the anecdotal level ! They don't seem to have any way of getting at the meaning ! They don't seem to care what a sentence means ! That doesn't interest them ! "

It may seem overbold to suggest that this failure is not unconnected with the sort of reading habits developed earlier. If early reading matter contains nothing for the young minds to bite on, why would we expect their teeth to grow strong ? Why do we wonder if the " more and better courses " of the history professor prove only so many more crusts for tender gums to mumble, or if they have to be made " better " by being so progressivly made easier that the college is doing only what the grades should have done ?

This is no place in which to discuss why these things are so or to ask why the habits and likings of the least reflective teachers should rule policy in matters so vital as this. (We don't leave their customary conceptions of diet undisturbed. It took knowledgeable outsiders to show that orange juice and whole meal are what children need. Customary preferences for white flour are not allowed to stand in the way.) Our question is rather : What can more reflective teachers, who are well aware of these evils, do ? What would be a better way of trying to teach reading, as the art of making out what sentences may be saying ? Specifically, can Basic, or the ideas behind Basic, be of any help in the undertaking ?

That question came up from the beginning of work on Basic. It was inevitable in view of the preoccupation with ambiguity, obscurity, and misunderstanding from which Basic took its start. A simplified pocket language may be expected to have many uses in teaching reading. But these possible uses of Basic, as a tool in teaching reading and as a technique for studying hard writing, soon showed themselves to require much inquiry and experimentation—especially when oversimple proposals began to be put forward. For example, the proposal that children should be taught Basic exclusively as their first mode of speech must be squashed ; so must the proposal that Basic should be exclusively talked in nursery schools. These are the proposals of the fanatic or of the enthusiastic experimenter, and as a rule belong to the magical view of Basic, as a not too well understood source of wonders. The embarrassment such expectations are to those who have a grounded belief that Basic can be useful may be noted. People are always popping up to denounce us for proposals we would never make. A recent book, since withdrawn, supposed that we wished to have only Basic taught in the schools of England ! We agree that the proposal would be monstrous ; but do not suffer any the less from the accusation. That is not what Basic is for, and it is, to repeat, never in place as a substitute for the fullest use of English any English speakers can make. If I seem to harp on this, the sympathetic reader will see why.

Basic has no magical powers. It is a tool with certain uses which derive openly and evidently from its construction. Like all tools, it can be misused. It is not a foolproof apparatus. It is more like a hammer than a nutcracker. It cannot be guaranteed to extract meanings from sentences undamaged. It is useful in cracking hard shells, but we have to learn how to use it. And that very learning is in a large measure its value. We learn how the kernel of meaning is related to its verbal container.

From the beginning, it was clear enough that merely to learn Basic, to learn how to translate passages in fuller English into Basic, using the resources of the limited medium to their utmost extent, was an admirable exercise both in reading and writing. And, for a while, the efforts of those who took up this side of the work were devoted to showing how this exercise worked and what it could do.[2] But it was not equally clear that such courses in Basic could become a practicable part of the school curriculum, at least in any near future. There are resistances to learning Basic for these purposes, which students of Basic well understand. We might be and were certain that those who did the necessary work (it is neither arduous nor prolonged) invariably found it amply repaying. But this did not show that those who most needed the help such work could give them could, in general, be persuaded to do it. In some school or college classes, teachers with the necessary ability and enthusiasm could and did work up their own materials and achieve striking success. Dr. Upton at Whittier and Dr. Tilley at the University of Connecticut are examples. In different ways they took Basic and made it a main instrument of their teaching. In general, however, guidance, texts, and a developed and graded programme were obviously

[2]See A. P. Rossiter's *Statement and Suggestion*, Hugh Walpole's *Semantics*, my *Basic in Teaching : East and West*, Chapter Eleven in my *Interpretation in Teaching ;* and, for application in advanced reading exercises, J. L. Sweeney's " Basic in Reading " in *The Kenyon Review*, Vol. V, No. 1 1943.

necessary if any extensive and satisfactory use of Basic in school or college curricula was to be made.

Let me first show briefly why some sort of work with Basic in school English classes is desirable and what it could do. Then we shall consider what is possible and how best it might be done.

The essential value of work with Basic lies in the kind and degree of attention it turns on to the text that is being translated or studied with its aid. This it shares with any other mode of translation or paraphrase *properly. used*. Its advantage over translation into foreign languages or paraphrase in full English is simply that Basic by the very limitations of its vocabulary keeps the proper use more constantly in sight.

But what is this proper use ? There is some difference of opinion about it among teachers. A recent statement by Mr. Frederick L. Santee on the point brings up many relevant considerations very clearly :

I have mentioned the use of Basic as a vehicle for paraphrasing and stressed the danger of assuming too readily that the Basic version is superior to the original. A teacher of English has just told me that he no longer has his students write paraphrases of difficult passages in Milton because they tend to like their own simpler restatements better than Milton's English. The value of paraphrasing consists not in showing the student the meaning of the original, but in showing the teacher whether or not the student knows it already. No student can paraphrase into his own basic, or translate either into the standard Basic or into any foreign language without first comprehending the passage with which he is dealing. Comprehension must come first, and it comes from explanation of words and phrases by the teacher, from careful, sympathetic study of the passage by the student, and from the use of dictionaries and commentaries. If the student can translate, he understands ; but the understanding, not the translation, is the teacher's aim. Translation is overworked in most foreign languages because it is mistaken for a means of teaching. Its proper place is in quizzes, written or oral.[3]

On the first point I am wholly with Mr. Santee. It would be disastrous indeed if students supposed that their Basic versions beat the original, except with examples chosen as richly deserving a beating. Most Basic versions, however, are not very likely to be long admired by their authors, and this danger may safely be assumed to be small.

As to the sad fate of Milton in that classroom, something in the

[3]" Basic, Latin, and Other Languages," *The Kenyon Review*, Vol. V, No. 1, 1943.

handling of the exercises must have gone very wrong. But the third sentence contains the point that needs to be focused. " The value of paraphrasing consists not in showing the student the meaning of the original, but in showing the teacher whether or not the student knows it already." That, it seems to me, takes much too distant a view of the process of paraphrasing. It sees paraphrasing as a mere putting down on paper of a meaning *already* perceived. " Knows it already " is the dangerous phrase. Paraphrasing, in its proper use, is not reporting, it is exploration. It is an experimental feeling around, a tasting and comparing of the possibilities of the original's meaning. With all passages that should be chosen for such paraphrasing work, these possibilities are richer, more varied than any one version of them can give. There is a suggestion throughout Mr. Santee's paragraph that " the meaning " of a passage is something fixed and separable, something like the right answer to a sum that can be worked out once and for all and then handed in, and even a suggestion that the values lie in the answers rather than in the processes of exploration and reflection by which we reach them. This may be unfair to Mr. Santee, but many teachers will certainly find such conceptions encouraged by his phrasing.

Even in studying mathematics, it is the development of mathematical insight and skill, not the answer that matters. In teaching reading this is as true. Not the product of understanding (some local meaning) but the process itself of working out the meanings is what we must keep our eye on. Translation and paraphrase are, of course, useful in quizzes : they let the teacher and the student see what has been misunderstood. But that is a subordinate use. The proper main use is in developing, through reflective exercise, the process of understanding.

This, I think, is the heart of the problem. The reason why people do not learn to read well is that too much of what exercise they get either puts up no problem to them or is merely anecdotal —or, at best, has no exploration of meaning but only some factual quiz in view. This has doubtless been said in various forms and incessantly since reading first began. Every candid reader, and every good teacher, knows it to be true. We all endeavour to remedy it by whatever means we may. Basic is one such means. Its peculiarity is that it forces you so constantly to explore into the meaning of the original. You cannot transpose it into Basic without close inquiry.

If we compare translation into Basic with translation into

Latin, on the one hand, and with paraphrase into full English on the other, we shall see why this is so. Translation into Latin is recognized to be a far finer exercise in understanding English than translation into French—because the differences between the Latin and English ways of saying things are so much greater. We can frequently translate almost word for word into French ; but to put a passage of English into Latin we have to separate the meaning from the English turns of phrase and set to work to rethink it in Latin terms. This makes us aware of the meaning (of the possibilities of meaning, rather) of the English to a degree in which putting it into French as a rule will not. But the values here for the improvement of our understanding *of English* depend obviously on how good our knowledge of Latin is. If we don't know enough Latin and don't know it well enough, the gain is slight ; we are just *wishing* a meaning on to a Latin dummy, and we can do that without looking at all carefully into the meaning. If we have a good teacher, the process helps to teach us Latin but it does not necessarily make us any better at grasping English. The same applies to translation into French. Translation into poorly understood media does not improve our understanding of the original. Most so-called translation used in schools and colleges as a part of elementary language learning is but mutual mayhem : both languages suffer alike. Nonetheless, translation into a *really well-understood* language, remote enough in its structure and habits from English, is the best training in the reading of English available. Unfortunately it is only available to good scholars in these languages.

If Latin is too difficult, full English is too easy. A process of " synonym trading " is not illuminating. Let me quote what I wrote on another occasion :

Paraphrases in general divide into two types. There is the paraphrase which merely replaces the words in the original with rough synonyms leaving all the doubtful parts of the meaning unillumined. This exercise of shuffling synonyms about is merely deadening to whatever germs of interpretative capacity may exist in the student. It is agreed that the less he is subjected to it the better.

But the alternative is almost as bad. Here to write a paraphrase is to compose another passage made as nearly as possible a rival to the first. As such, it is an exercise whose effects are often very far indeed from an improved comprehension of the original. This is the kind of paraphrase the more promising kind of pupil usually produces and he deserves our sympathy. For the terms of the task set him are something of an outrage on his intelligence. He is given an original which presumably he res-

D

pects ; he is asked—under the unfair condition that he may use none of the best words because these have been used already by the original —to build up a cluster of words, which will, so far as he can contrive, be an equivalent. The better reader he is, the more closely will he realize that what he is being asked to do is something not only presumptuous but impossible and absurd.[4]

Basic avoids these defects by not, as a rule, having the rough synonyms and the second-best words. It forces the reader to start again and think through what he supposes the original to have said. And he has to think it through in other terms—not so far removed as those of Latin but further than those of French. As Mr. Santee well remarks, " . . . the Basic version requires more careful study and better understanding of the original than the French does, but much less than the Latin does. For practical purposes translation into French requires too little examination of the meaning ; translation into Latin requires too much. . . . I wish," he continues, " the promoters of Basic would select for translation the most pompous and verbose books and flaunt their Basic versions before the faces of all young writers. In this way Basic might have a salutary effect on English style." Even without so self-sacrificing a programme, we find that it does.

Mr. Santee offers an example : " For the greater glory of Basic, here is a specimen meant to show how English ought not to be written.

The apperception of self-motivation is a psychological fact. A concomitant phenomenon is the consciousness that the origin of this motivation is internal and not external."

In Basic this might be :

The mind is conscious that it is self-moving ; and, at the same time, that the motion comes from inside itself, not from outside.

Or, letting *apperception* take more of its traditional meanings :

After and through experience the mind becomes able to do things—in place of having them done to it. That is a fact with whatever degree of authority we let the facts of " psychology " have. And together with this power of acting for or from itself comes, so it seems, the knowledge that this is so.

It will be seen that Basic allows us ample scope in our inter-

[4] *Basic in Teaching : East and West*, Kegan Paul, London, 1935, pp. 56-7.

pretation of such things. The liberty *here*—and " the appercep-tion of self-motivation " is another phrase for freedom—feels indeed as wide as we could wish. Using Basic for our paraphrase does not hold us down to any one interpretation or narrow the range of the different meanings we may find. Basic, indeed, is inherently broad in its handling and may be compared to charcoal rather than to a hard pencil. Such breadth—as teachers of draw-ing know—has its disadvantages as well as its merits ; it may, for a brief moment, encourage some to confuse a smudge with a statement. But to balance against this, width of treatment is peculiarly suggestive : it forces us to decide *which* of the features, aspects, interpretations of the original we are going to portray or indicate. It makes us aware, as no tighter, more precise medium can, that the original *has* these different possibilities to offer, that in all reading *we* are selecting meanings, not passively taking the stamp, and that we have a responsibility to choose well. In brief, it makes us take this " apperception of self-motivation " seriously.

It is through this that Basic can help us to become better rea-ders—through heightening our sense of what we are doing as we read. In most reading we are intent, and quite rightly, on the particular meaning at that point of the passage. We are not reminding ourselves of the possibility that the passage may mean something more, something quite other, perhaps, than we have yet supposed. We are not reflecting on our possible losses. Like dogs with our noses to the ground we are too busy to look up and see the other game that may be standing in full view. Nothing blinds us so well as a prepossession, and in most reading we are prepossessed. The cure is in realizing that this is so. Comparing Basic versions is a good way of waking ourselves up. We see how easily we suppose that an author must be trying to say certain things, when in fact nothing of that sort was in his mind at all.

" The true mode of interpretation," said Aristotle in the *Poetics* with everlasting truth, " is the precise opposite of what Glaucon mentions. Critics, he says, jump at certain groundless conclusions ; they pass judgment and then proceed to reason on it ; and assuming that the poet has said whatever they happen to think, find fault if a thing is inconsistent with their own fancy." It is this trick of assuming that what we happen to think is the only thing the passage can be saying that betrays us all. Then the very things that might show us that we were wrong—the in-consistencies—become faults in the author.

This hasty leaping to groundless conclusions and the disputatious spirit that goes with it are the chief enemies of good reading in more advanced studies. We want to uphold or attack a certain point. We care more deeply about the point—about the attack or defence—than about whether what we read really presents it. We are more willing to be soothed by what we take as support, or to be roused by what we take as offence, than to inquire, reflect, and consider. Inquiry, reflection, and consideration are far higher activities of the mind than verbal self-comfort or verbal warfare. They are harder to keep up, more tiring, more of a strain on our " self-motivation." We need to be more ourselves in them, and they are the way, in fact, by which we become more ourselves. In comparison, argument, debate and dispute are ways of losing ourselves, of " being moved (positively or negatively) from without."

Unluckily a very strong strand in our Western tradition will have it that debate is the very heartbeat of inquiry and that it is by contention and dispute that we winnow the grain of truth from the chaff. We are aggressive, intellectually, rather than meditative. We admire the " vigorous " thinker—by which we usually mean the argumentative rather than the deep one. " Meditation," indeed, suggests to us a faint activity : the conduct of a sissy in thought. We are mistaken in this. Meditation should mean for us a closer, more continuous, a wider and more experimental thinking, turning the matter over more and examining more of its sides and possibilities. We badly need a retraining that will break our habit of " jumping at groundless conclusions." It is because Basic offers us a technique for such retraining that it has an interesting future in education.

" Certainly one *quality*, which nowadays has been best forgotten—and that is why it will take some time yet for my writings to become readable—is essential if we are to practise reading as an art," said Nietzsche, " a quality for the exercise of which it is necessary to be a cow, and under *no circumstances* a modern man !—rumination."[5] The making of Basic versions is training in rumination, in chewing the cud, in preparing what we read for digestion. Digestion, dyspeptics apart, is no manner of warfare. All the words we use in describing thought have interesting

[5]At the end of the preface to *The Genealogy of Morals*. A cow is very different from " the beast of prey, the magnificent *blonde brute* avidly rampant for spoil and victory," he elsewhere, as in the First Essay there, so much admired.

suggestions as to what we should be doing in it. When we *consider*, that word brings in the stars—the widest framework of reference ; when we *deliberate* or *ponder*, we are weighing and balancing (not fighting) ; when we *revolve* a matter in our minds, we turn it over ; when we *reflect* upon it, we try different angles or slants. All these are pacific activities. The exception is the word *argue*. This may have originally meant " to keep on making clear " (it comes from Old French *arguer* which came from the Latin *argutare*, the frequentative of *arguere*, to make clear) but in most of its many uses, is that what the word now means ? Is that what arguing usually aims at or achieves ? Most arguments, alas, rather follow the course that Glaucon so well described. We argue to maintain or contend, not to discover more fully what it is we are maintaining or contending against.

Basic as a tool in training thought discourages dispute. It curbs our eternal temptation to argue before we know what we are arguing about. It is a restraint upon that habit of verbal warfare which may be connected more closely than we suppose with actual warfare as a key institution of our traditional culture. We shall never have a reasonable world until we are more reasonable within ourselves. While we think that it is the chief business of ideas (and ideologies) to fight with one another in our minds, we should not be surprised if men behave as though their chief business were to fight with one another. The inner and the outer warfare are connected. But our ideas have more important things to do than to make war on one another, just as men and nations have more important things to do. They have to find out about one another, adjust themselves together in a wider order, and breed a better race of ideas to take their place. Basic, rightly used, can help, we believe, in this. It can bring ideas to terms with one another, keep them from so readily mistaking one another, from supposing too soon that what seems incompatible and hostile must be so. But that " rightly used " is important. Neither Basic nor any other instrument of thought can do this automatically. It is no substitute for thought ; it is only a means of inducing favourable opportunities for better thinking.

Here I must touch on the question : " How hard is Basic for those to whom English is their native language ? " It will be seen that this is less a single question than a swarm of them. If it asks " How hard is it to travel, shop, visit, do the daily routine business in Basic ? " a few hours' study and practice are enough.

I discuss the matter at some length in the chapter that follows. If it asks " How hard is it to say things in the best available way in Basic ? " that needs a more elaborate answer. How hard is it to say things in the best available way in full English ? That plainly depends on what the things are, for whom they are said, and the knack and training of the man who is to say them. Deep down, I suppose it turns upon how thoroughly we *understand* what we are trying to say, and how thoroughly we understand English. Most of us who use English really understood it very slightly, or understand it well only at certain levels and in certain ranges of its uses. A good popular writer understands it as most people will best use it. A philosopher may better understand its deeper and more complex uses, but fail utterly with it at popular levels. Shakespeare could understand and use all English at all levels.

So, too, with Basic versions. No one can make good Basic versions if he does not in the first place understand his Basic words and sentences well and, secondly, contrive somehow to understand the original he is translating. And that is a task of inquiry, consultation, and reflection and as such takes time. Basic can help in this remarkably—by bringing out points that are not being understood, by raising relevant questions, and by delaying conclusions. Through the very fact that its vocabulary is so limited, we are forced, as we practice with it, to become aware of the varying implications of its words. It becomes a segment of the language we understand so well that it puts us on our guard against the rest of the language *and itself*. But there is, once again, no self-acting virtue in Basic, though too many people seem to think there should be. Putting something into Basic does *not* automatically clarify it. Why so many people should suppose that it does is a question worth asking. Probably they are expecting words to do their thinking for them. Some, for example, have been disappointed to discover that the Basic Dictionary does not somehow tell them what " the real meaning " of the words they look up is ! They seem to have hoped that Basic could be a sort of linguistic machine into which they could feed difficult English and have it come out in crystal-clear and easy sentences.

That is a mistake, plainly enough. So is the idea that Basic itself is committed to some one philosophy. It is a means for exploring all philosophies and all questions. Different users will, of course, handle it with their own presuppositions, but

Basic itself is a neutral set of tools. No one need fear that the use of Basic imposes any special tendency on thought, or assumes any *parti pris*, or any tendency more special than the encouragement of investigation before a decision as to what anything may or may not mean.

This suggests that most things worth study are likely to mean more than one thing. It is so. Our job in reading is not simply to find one meaning—*the* meaning. It is to see as clearly as we can what the meanings are that may most reasonably be given to the passage. The proof of this is the historic fact that just those remarks that have been most important (have " meant most ") to man have led to the most discussion as to what they say. " The Kingdom of Heaven is within you " and " Virtue is knowledge " are good examples. But the key sentences of most treaties, judgments, or business proposals illustrate the point, too.

There are opportunities here for grand-scale verbal battles. I have written recently of them at length,[6] hoping to induce a more meditative and peaceful exploration of the problem. Any such suggestion, of course, arouses the combative man. It is a way of stealing his enemy from him which he cannot forgive—until he lays his argumentative weapons down and begins to think in other fashions. So Mr. Elder Olson, for example, in *Modern Philology*, has dubbed my remarks " dangerous nonsense," an honour they did not seek. " In the first place there must be one and only one right reading, because meaning—if we intend by that the meaning of the philosopher and not the infinite and unpredictable reactions of his readers—may be manifold but never multiple, from the very nature of signification : if x stands for what is x and what is not x, x stands for everything and nothing."

This is disputation of the type which work with Basic versions discourages. Mr. Olson speaks with feeling of my " appalling translations of Aristotle and Whitehead in the eternal Basic." Equally disputatious would be the reply that if Mr. Olson were right, I, as the author of the challenged remarks, would be uniquely placed to tell him just how much he misrepresented the views he professed to be attacking. But that would be vain warfare, the worst way of trying to clarify the situation. I fear a reference to Aristotle and Glaucon in the passage I have cited above would do Mr. Olson little good. It is far wiser to leave him to fence with his dummies and consider peaceably whether

[6]In *How to Read a Page*, especially pp. 11-12.

it is not true that sentences often have meanings different from those the author may have intended. As author he is reponsible for any meanings which reasonable (undisputatious) readers give them after taking into account the other things he says and whatever else is most relevant. Good and understanding reading then becomes a matter of taking these relevant things into account. It is interpretation in the literal or etymological sense of the word—a taking of the remark together with the rest which bears upon it. And, as practice with Basic, or any other mode of translation that makes us think enough, will bring out, we have, as a rule, to deliberate not one but several possible meanings. Such deliberation leads to understanding *of the subject*. To be given, by some authority, a cut and dried meaning for the remarks—even if it happens to be right—does not. We are back here at the quiz conception of understanding—a knowledge of the answer which does not depend on clear perception of the question.

This is the key point about the use of Basic in education. Do we or do we not favour the quiz-kid type of learning as an equipment for life ? Is it quality of understanding and reflection, or acquaintance with facts available in *The World Almanac*, in encyclopædias, and other works of reference, which we would put in the forefront among our aims. I do not believe an educator worth the name will disagree about the answer. The doubt will only be about the means by which understanding and reflection can best be encouraged. And I can only say that the experience of all those who have yet made any persistent experimentation with Basic as a stimulant to reflection is that it is a useful aid.

The question remains : How may it be made most useful ? There are several schools of thought. Some are convinced of the value of translation into *strict* Basic—with suitably chosen passages. They believe that the very rigidity and definiteness of the specification of strict Basic give us a peculiar opportunity to set tasks demanding a sharp awareness in the student of what he may and may not do *within the rules*. Too few of our studies, they believe, require such exact observance of rules. The rules do not matter, they might say ; what matters is that we should know whether we are keeping to them or not.

On the other hand there are those who believe that some of these rules are unnecessary and undesirable for this use of Basic. They were introduced with the foreign learner in view, to make his passage into English smoother. They are no aid to the student who knows English already as his mother tongue. And, on this view, they get in the way of more important things. While remembering, for example, to say " give an organization to " in place of " organize " he may neglect to consider sufficiently what " organize " and " organization " may mean. This view favours a modification of the Rules of Basic to allow the use of all verbs represented by or contained in the Basic nouns, the use of certain suffixes such as—*full* and *-ness*, and sundry other enlargements. But it holds to the Basic List as the foundation of the paraphrasing vocabulary. To enlarge that would be to lose the power to provoke thought which its very limitations give to Basic.

A third view goes further and proposes to hand over to the student the task of making and defending his own rules. Let him go outside the Basic List wherever the task of keeping within it raises no interesting point of interpretation. Words like *canary*, *pavement*, *precipice*, for example, will in most sentences raise no questions worth special attention. Let them be used freely then, though they are not important enough to be Basic words. But let the responsibility of deciding which words are in this comfortable, unquestionable position be fully faced and carried by the student. Let him be sure that all words that *do* raise problems of meaning—whether they are on the Basic List or not —get proper attention and clarification in his version.[7]

The principle behind this policy is that we should always in this sort of work be as fully aware as possible of what we are doing and why we are doing it. As Aristotle said, the highest, most human activity of the mind is that in which it both *makes* and *keeps* its rules. Relatively blind adherence to rules worked out by others may be a necessary training for this freedom, but to profit from any sort of freedom we need constant exercise in the responsibilities it entails. Practice in our judgment as to how far we have found and overcome the difficulties of exposition is one of its most valuable forms. This third policy concentrates upon giving such practice.

It will be evident that between these three policies there is plenty of room for experiment. Probably they form a series ; some work with strict Basic seems a desirable introduction to work with a more supple medium, which would lead into the freedom of the third policy. It is still too early to make any

[7] I have discussed this view in some detail in *How to Read a Page*, Chapter Seven.

D*

report. Without texts, which have still to undergo much revision and development, there would be no point in going into detail.[8] The aim throughout is clear and simple : concentration upon those problems in handling language, for the benefit of thought, which are likely to be of the widest general profit to the learner. Some of the difficulties of reading and writing are local. When we have mastered them we have mastered nothing more. But others are general ; they recur with slight variations incessantly, and if we succeed in overcoming them in a number of varying examples we win power over countless parallel problems. We have learned something universal in the art of thinking through words.[9] Basic, in its various uses, can, we believe, be a very good means of directing attention upon just these problems. That is the whole claim. Needless to repeat, I hope, no one wants Basic to replace the fuller use of English in the education of English-speaking people. Its aim here is only to make that fuller use more adequate and more discerning than it is.

There are, however, a number of more immediate applications of Basic and Basic technique to problems of communication which must be mentioned. All those who are under urgent necessity to explain complex matters to untrained readers know very well how hard it is to get information, instruction, and advice to them in a serviceable form. Whether it concerns the rulings of the Office of Price Administration, income-tax regulations, how to take down ball bearings, or larger matters of national and international policy, the loss of efficiency incurred through failure in communication is a nightmare. Those most engaged with the practical aspects of such work know best how great the waste is. It has occurred to many that Basic may have some help to give here, and questions have in fact been asked in the House of Commons and other parliaments on this point—sometimes as a way of criticizing government statements, more often with a wholly serious intent.

An answer cannot be quite simple. A proposal that rulings, explanations, and the rest intended for the lay public and the untrained reader be merely translated into Basic would certainly be over simple. After all, the people these communications are

[8] Some experimental photo-offset materials are in preparation and may be obtained from the Harvard Commission on English Language Studies.

[9] A fuller treatment of this topic will be found in *Interpretation in Teaching*, Kegan Paul, 1938.

addressed to are speakers of English, however much the technicality or the complexity of the matters talked of may find and leave them at a loss. A Basic version would be artificial for such readers ; it would simplify (as for the foreign learner) at points where simplification is, for the native speaker of English, unnecessary and may even be distracting. And at other points additional clarification might well be needed. As I have insisted above, there is nothing automatic or mechanical about the elucidatory powers of Basic. The only way to use it to clear up a difficulty is by understanding clearly what the difficulty is. We cannot rely on Basic, or on anything else, to do that for us.

Nonetheless, in such work of clarification, Basic has, we believe, an important part to play. The making of a rough Basic version (which need not necessarily aim to be 100 per cent Basic) is an extremely good preparation for drafting a statement or explanation designed to be as clear as possible for as many people as possible. For the reasons entered into above, it forces a rethinking of the subject matter, and this is very often the key to success. When the rough Basic version has been made, its adaptation to a form that will go home most smoothly, most forcibly, and least ambiguously to the audience is usually no great undertaking. It still needs, of course, adequate understanding of the subject matter and enough imagination to realize what range of ideas about *that* the audience is likely to command. This last, as the most experienced will be the first to admit, is the qualification hardest to attain. The good popularizer has it, as the technician and expert have the special knowledge. Basic can often serve as the bridge between them.

Instances of such uses of Basic might be given from many fields.[10] The following experiment in making public-health information more widely available and effective is typical.

Mrs. Gwendolyn C. Lee, a medical social worker in the Slossfield Health Centre of Birmingham, Alabama, was the instigator. About five hundred Negro patients come each week to this clinic, and most of them receive little pamphlets intended to help them with their health problems both as individuals and as collaborators in public-health measures. Mrs. Lee suspected that these pamphlets, although written for a mass audience, were considerably above the heads of this group. She knew that

[10]See, for instance, a discussion of the Bill of Rights, for a teacher's use, by J. L. Sweeney, printed in *The Bill of Rights Review*, Vol. II, No. II, Winter, 1942.

they were misunderstood and feared that they were found so difficult by the patients that after trying one they would never attempt to read another. She asked her husband, who had been studying Basic in a seminar at the University of Chicago, whether Basic might help.

Mr. Lee, being also of a scientific habit of mind, decided to investigate. He took four typical pamphlets : *Information for Expectant Mothers*, *Health Almanac*, *The Care of the Teeth*, and a reprint from the *Reader's Digest* entitled " Why Don't We Stamp Out Syphilis ? "   From these he chose typical paragraphs expressing some of their central ideas. Under each of them he placed six statements in Basic that could be marked " true " or " false " on the basis of what the paragraph said. Then, in a separate booklet, he gave near-Basic versions of the same paragraphs—using a few non-Basic words like *mosquito* and *syphilis* and adjusting them freely to the comprehension of the audience in the manner described above. Under these simplified versions, he put the same instructions and test statements as before.

Mrs. Lee then selected two groups of her patients, matching them as carefully as possible person by person. She set aside those able to read both the original and the simple version adequately and those who could do nothing with either. This left sixty-five persons available for the experiment. One group read the original and the other the simple version. Both were allowed all the time they wanted to complete the test. Here are the results :

Readers of the original took on the average twenty-three minutes ; the " Basic " group took on the average fifteen minutes. The middle score of the " original " group was eleven out of twenty-four test sentences marked correctly ; the middle score of the " Basic " group was 17.9

These facts seem of very general interest. Our public-health authorities and other agencies give away annually many millions of pamphlets intended to help people to deal with common and serious problems. Yet these people, to put it roughly, seem to have understood less than half of what they read in the original version, even though they devoted on an average about *six minutes* to each short paragraph and were forced by the test to consider more carefully than usual what it said. Through the simple device of translation into near-Basic—even by a novice, for Mr. Lee had had no previous experience in this sort of work —their reading time was cut down by a third and their understanding of what they read was increased by 60 per cent.

In most cases no such quantitative evidence of the gain in efficiency will be available. We must rely upon our own impressions. Here, from a very different field—the exposition of democratic principle—is an example of Basic at work, on which the reader must be his own judge.

The following is from page 94 of Mr. R. B. Perry's recent *Shall Not Perish from the Earth*. It comes from toward the end of a short, highly compressed book and is clearly a summary— something we should not expect to understand very fully except by reference to what has gone before.

There can be no doubt of the profound antithesis between totalitarianism and the traditional creed of Americans. As these four ideas, uniformitarianism, anti-intellectualism, tribalism, and technologism, give meaning to totalitarianism, so do their opposites define democracy, as a whole composed of individualism, rationalism, universalism, and moral purposiveness.

What I have done with it is to make as short a Basic version of it as I could which would put the ideas it is handling, which are set forth in Mr. Perry's book, into a form ready—or readier—for discussion.

There will be no doubt that " totalitarianism " is the very opposite of those ways of belief and of living which have been handed down to us from the American past. Four ideas together make up " totalitarianism." They are :

1. *Uniformitarianism*—the idea that all men *are to be made as completely the same* as possible, in the interests of society.

2. *Anti-intellectualism*—the idea that men are to be guided through their uncontrolled feelings, and chiefly through their desires, hates, and fears, not through thought and reason.

3. *Tribalism*—the idea that the group is to be given the belief that they are somehow all of the same blood, a better blood than any other, and that it is right for men of this higher blood to have power over all others.

4. *Technologism*—the idea that power, especially machine power and the control of natural forces, is the great end, and that man is the servant of power.

The opposites of these ideas together make up democracy. They are :

1. *Individualism*—the belief that *man's end or good* (the thing for him to go after) is to become *as completely himself as possible*, with the fullest development of all his powers in all the ways that will let him get on with other men for his good and their good as men living together in society.

2. *Rationalism*—the belief that thought and reason—not feelings or desires—are the right guides for man in all his decisions.

3. *Universalism*—the belief that the good of *every* man—not of oneself only or of any group, but of all men equally whoever they are—is the right end to be kept in view in all men's doings.

4. *Moral Purposiveness*—the belief that all other purposes and all uses of power are only important as instruments in the great design of putting men into harmony with one another for their common good.

This is an expansion in strict Basic, from which a statement could be worked up to any degree thought desirable. What " thought " and " reason " might be saying would, of course, be the crux of any discussion, and on that there is no better guide than Plato's *Republic*. The abridged version founded on Basic is an example of what may be done through Basic to make the best that has been thought and said on the most urgent matters available most simply to everyone.[11]

Our leading men, the press, the radio, the journals of discussion and education, have been vying with one another to deplore the fact that youth is not interested in democracy, does not take it seriously, does not " believe in it," no longer feels about it as its fathers and mothers felt. If this is a fact, it certainly marks a turning point in history. But there is another possible explanation. Young people might just not *understand the ideas* about man, his freedoms and his duties, which all talk and writing about democracy must use. These are not to be taken in clearly and kept clear by minds unpractised in reflection. They need thoughts. They are not facts about how people actually behave—which might be memorized along with other facts and formulas. They are *ideas*—in the sense of necessities of the moral order ; but any attempt to say what they are inevitably raises all the hardest problems. It may well be that this seemingly indifferent youth suspects that these hardest of all hard questions wait here, suspects that much of the loudest talk about democracy ignores them, and that most of the talkers do not even attempt to understand them. Better silence than lip worship, if so. What we would be witnessing, then, would not be a turning away from democracy as a thing examined and found wanting, but just a healthy if fearful avoidance of such doctrines by those who have not been taught how to understand them. They would be right to accompany the avoidance with an icy distrust of all who

[11]Some further materials for such a discussion are collected in *How to Read a Page*, Chapters Six and Seven.

suppose that doctrine we dare not examine and are not ready to live up to can help us.

The problem then would be, how are these generations to be equipped, fortified, and encouraged to think as deeply as may be about such matters ?   If they are not helped they will have suffered the worst of betrayals, and the whole world will have been betrayed through them.   Democratic principles are not a separable subject.   More and better courses on them will only make matters worse still.   Any persistent thought about man and his ways—and that covers all the humanities—forwards their understanding.   The humanities indeed are a vanity in so far as they do not lead toward that.   They are no mere records of fact, once again.   They are a series of ever new understandings. It is the art of understanding we come back to, the skill with meanings we call intelligence.   How can we cultivate that ?

Chapter Seven

IMMEDIATE APPLICATIONS

MOST of my readers will be neither statesmen nor teachers of language. But what I have been saying has addressed itself to the statesman and the teacher latent in every man. We are citizens of a world in which no hand that can help can be spared, if we are to put it into any better order. The next ten years will be a turning point. Most of us, if we are to help, will have to change some of our ways of living and habits of thought and take up new responsibilities. They will be no hardships. The hard thing would be to find no way to help. " A man who does not say to himself ' What to do ! What to do ! '—indeed I do not know what to do with such a person," said Confucius, who lived in even more hopeless-seeming times than ours. It is worth recalling that Confucius was, to the keeper of the Stone Gate, " the fellow who knows that a thing cannot be done and still wants to do it."[1] The heartening fact is that he did it. He gave a way of life to China that is still one of the chief assurances that a saner world is possible.

Among ways of taking a share in the work is the furtherance of a world language. But if much is to be done we must not see that as a job for experts and technicians only. It is everybody's business every bit as much as public health is a joint concern of us all. The medical profession has its special duty, but without wide co-operation it cannot raise or extend our level of physical well-being much. We have to join in by watching and controlling our ways of living, and to do that we have to inform ourselves in some measure.[2] Is it too much to suggest that those who want the general levels of communication to be raised and extended should do likewise ? That they should be ready to watch and control on occasion some of their ways of expressing themselves ?

This is no proposal that we should all talk Basic. Heaven forbid ! No one who knows Basic will willingly confine himself

[1] Lin Yutang's translation in *The Wisdom of China and India*.
[2] Another parallel might be the control of rumour and unhelpful comment on the motives or behaviour of other nations in wartime. That is the special business of offices of information, but they must work by enlisting general co-operation.

to it—except for special purposes. It is only the suggestion that a widespread knowledge of its principles and a little skill in it among those who have to do with learners of English would be an immense help. In a very real sense everyone in contact with those who are struggling with our language is both a statesman and a teacher. It is to the common interest if he equips himself for the undertaking.

How hard is Basic English for an English speaker to learn? Mr. Wells, our most audacious modern prophet, in *The Shape of Things to Come* (1933) did not let himself be optimistic in dating the general use of Basic. Here is what he said : " One of the unanticipated achievements of the twenty-first century was the rapid diffusion of Basic English as the lingua franca of the world."

One reason for such a late date may have been Mr. Wells's notion (which many people seem to share) that Basic must be very hard for English-speaking people to use. He even goes to the trouble of inventing a certain teacher of languages, named Rudolph Boyle, who " contrived the method by which English speakers learned to confine themselves, when necessary, to Basic limitations." Experience shows that there is in fact no considerable difficulty and little need for any special training. A few hours spent in serious study of the principles, and a little practice, enable most people to write fairly freely in something near enough to strict Basic for all practical purposes. Reading one or two stories or chapters in Basic, some experiments in rephrasing paragraphs of ordinary English, followed by study of good Basic versions of these paragraphs, and a spell of free composition in Basic will do the trick. *The General Basic English Dictionary* is a ready aid in trouble. It will not, of course, give us always the answer to our problem in any mechanical fashion. No dictionary could possibly do that, though there are always some victims of educational malpractice who go on all their lives hoping that reference books will think for them. But it will suggest *strong belief* as a substitute for *conviction*, and *unnecessary* or *of no use* for *otiose* ; it will help us to see that *to tolerate a person* may be *to put up with him* and *to tolerate a thing*, perhaps, is *to let it go on without protest*. In most instances, however, the explanation will resist transplanting neatly into an aperture left by a non-Basic word to be avoided. A recasting of the sentence will, as a rule, be necessary. It is this very failure to get a word by word substitution which helps us to ask ourselves again just what we are saying and why.

Impromptu eloquence and after-dinner wit in Basic are tougher assignments. Its thrifty vocabulary is at its best in everyday dealings and explanations, and is not naturally a spell-binder's medium. In a continuous, extemporary speech in Basic one has to pause a moment between remarks to see how the next sentence is coming out. But in practice, for any audience for whom it is really important to use Basic, a close approximation to Basic is sufficient to make all the difference between being well-enough understood and not. A demonstration speech made chiefly to prove that one *can* say it in Basic (where there is no other good reason for refraining from obvious words) is always something of a strain. It is, and feels like, a tour de force. The proper condition for good communication—one's sense of the needs and understanding of the audience—is lacking. So, too, with some writing in Basic—the sort which as far as possible aspires to hide the fact that a limited language is being used. These are showpieces, not the normal use of the medium. Students of Basic, however, rarely escape a sojourn in this trap. As skill and experience grow, Basic seems to challenge one for a time to display its paces, and the result is parade-ground stuff rather than standard riding.

Most people, however, become skilled enough with surprising ease. Mr. Wells's teacher-to-come reminds me, indeed, of the story about the man who got on the train with a strangely shaped basket. The old lady sitting opposite was much puzzled. After a while she said, " Would you think me too curious if I inquired what you have in your basket ? " " Not at all. It's a mongoose." Pause. " May I ask what the mongoose is for ? " " Why, I have an aunt who suffers from delusions. The poor dear thinks she is infested with snakes. The mongoose is to catch the snakes." Longer pause. " But didn't I understand you to say that the snakes were imaginary ? " " Yes, madam," said the man with the basket, " purely imaginary ; but so, you see, is the mongoose." Mr. Wells's difficulties and his Rudolph Boyle who is to catch them are equally imaginary.

Just how difficult Basic English may be as a foreign language, for different types of learners with different mother tongues under different conditions and aided by different teachers and learning aids, is not so readily ascertained. All that is certain, as yet, is that from China to Denmark, from the languages furthest from English to those nearest, for classes and those who teach themselves alike, a far more serviceable command of English has been gained in far less time than by any other plan. Very able young people who concentrate with determination can get through Basic into fuller English within a few weeks. The time has been cut, under exceptional circumstances (during a voyage, for example) to a few days. Elderly students who are unaccustomed to mental effort, and find concentration difficult, make incredibly more progress into Basic than into a less stream-lined course, even when they continue to treat their biweekly classes rather as an occasion for social relaxation than for toil. The earnest adult with little time to spare for his studies is, of course, grateful for the small memory load and orderly progress into English that the system permits.

Concentration, as much recent work on language learning indicates, is the key to the task. Five well-spaced-out separate hours a day for a month will do more than two hours a week for a whole year. Estimates in terms of total hours are somewhat meaningless here. Everything depends on how the hours are used, how they are spaced, how fresh the wits are, and what are the general incentives and immediate stimuli. The very usual school programme of four hours a week is not effective—for the earlier stages, at least. An intensive month at the start would economize effort immensely in the long run, and release time for other subjects later on.

The confident advance into fuller English and other subjects (including other languages) which able students of Basic make is memorable to those who have watched it. J.F., age sixteen, who had no knowledge of English at all when he joined his first class in Basic, three years later completed his sophomore year at his university with a grade of 92 in English. Such young Italians or Greeks must attend adult-education classes for language instruc-tion before they go to school in the ordinary way. They are sometimes surprised by the verbal disabilities of native English speakers. Too many of the classmates they later leave behind in high-school English cannot talk intelligently or read with compe-tence in their own language. Reference to its structure frightens or bores them. Questions of usage send them repeatedly and incuriously to a book of arbitrary rulings—with no better aim than to make their " papers " acceptable to teachers' standards which are unintelligible to them. Lucidity, force, or grace are ideas beyond their apprehension. Why one way of saying some-thing should be better than another is a question they have never seriously asked. All that they can do is to memorize, vainly, the forms which the teacher's corrections indicate to be right. That attempt made without understanding is foredoomed to failure. They sit imprisoned within impalpable walls, with very little hope—so every instructor in freshman English will agree—of ever winning out into the bright, intelligible reaches of their native tongue.

Such students cannot help beginners in English much. Though its means are limited, Basic is not a language for limited minds or limited interests. It lends itself to daily practical needs ; but it lends itself, too, and especially, to general discussion of the most important ideas which a world society must come to terms with. This makes it a means of helping planetary purposes as opposed to sectional aims, of easing tensions due to ignorance, of making the interdependence of peoples more manifest, of widening and enriching mutual awareness, and of consolidating world opinion against disruptive strains. A secondary language that became truly universal, carrying common news, common science, and, not least, common political ideas, their discussion and application, would—it needs no showing—help to defend us against future universal wars. That is the inducement which circumstances stress at this moment. But fear is a repulsion. It is not enough to be afraid of what we may do to one another ; we must be more imaginative and fall in love with the constructive possibilities. How little of human talent has ever yet been channelled to other than local aims. To turn a world language into an actuality we must see it as a way of remaking man.

The convenience to a traveller of finding everywhere people able to comprehend him cannot be overlooked. But the notion of the uses of a world language is inadequate. A man's ability to buy a hat in six languages does not in itself make him a better world citizen. The mere possession of a second language—regardless of the uses made of it—is an advantage, undoubtedly ; but we need not exaggerate its value. Only in so far as the second language deepens a mind's powers, does it become truly worth having. Only in so far as it becomes another organ of the spirit, through which other meanings are apprehended, and their otherness understood, is it certainly enlarging. When it gives no more than a dimmer version of what we already understand fully enough in our vernacular, it becomes a practical convenience only—by no means to be undervalued, but not the sort of thing to lead to a new humanity.

For many language students—as teachers grow tired of complaining—the tourist's conception of a language is dominant. The language remains a mere means of repeating the same things in another code. And it is too often assumed that only an advanced knowledge of a language can be a liberating knowledge. That is a mistake ; the liberation and enlargement of thought depend rather upon *how*—with what understanding —the language is learned than upon *how much* of it is picked up. A small segment of a language, well learned with its meanings well explored, is more valuable—from this point of view, as allowing one to see how its thought patterns compare with those of one's vernacular—than a larger vocabulary learned as a code. If our world secondary language is to tell us what other people are thinking, instead of letting us lend them our own thoughts, or hang our suspicions upon them, this aspect must be kept in mind. Great though the practical utility of *any* common medium is, there are greater values still to be attained if the medium really favours a genuine meeting of minds. We must not neglect the practical conveniences—as aids in so many of our other concerns, transport, trade, and the rest—but, for the growth of a world consciousness, *depth* of mutual understanding is paramount. All reflective students of languages agree on this. I wish I could assume that all extant teachers do. But below the highest ranges of the profession the code conception of a language is strong. Schedules, tests, and examinations fight for it. Demands for acquaintanceship with a multitude of words push ahead. Most teachers know how hard it is, under their pressure, to put understanding first—before the blank production of a generally " right enough " code answer.

Basic by its constitution leans to the side of understanding. With its stress on insight rather than rote memory, its preference for visibles and demonstrables in its key teaching patterns, its cultivation of metaphor, its avoidance of the bilingual dictionary, its practice of exploring more advanced English by means of simpler English—Basic relies on " thinking in English " as its main technique. It fights the code conception by the very economy of its vocabulary. Translating into Basic, as we have seen, is a rethinking of the meaning, not a one-for-one replacement of words. And this rethinking has to be in English. Thus, competence in Basic is favourably inclined to the sort of meeting of minds which better human relations require.

The understanding a beginner in a language establishes with

his teacher is often especially close. So again is it when he first tries out his growing powers in friendly converse with others. If the native speakers are able to come to meet the beginner, there is the opportunity for a peculiar relation of mutual aid in the joint endeavour to maintain communication. The one is struggling to express something—the others to understand it and reply. Their success is a common triumph. An unusual candour on both sides, a simplicity which is not merely linguistic, often accompanies such efforts. Men then return to a fresher world in which the miracle of speech has regained its glory, become conscious again of the tenuousness and fragility of human contacts, and are readier to enjoy and honour them with sincerity and a fuller sense of what we owe them. Greater linguistic accomplishment dulls these feelings. Language becomes once more a way of concealing our thoughts, of preserving conventional social relations. But the first stages of a beginner's progress are often lit by moments of peculiarly intimate communion— if he is fortunate in those he encounters.

They in their turn have been privileged. But they have another privilege : that of keeping to their own language, of which they have probably been keenly aware. And this privilege imposes a duty : of being more alert to what their words will mean, of being more supple and appropriate in their choices, of being less ready to hand over the responsibility for being understood, of being more aware of assumptions, and so on.

No doubt, being able to help beginners to talk with us is in part a knack ; in part it depends on what is called a sympathetic temperament and patience ; but it can be greatly heightened by reflection, and by that kind of study of the difficulties of our language which is exemplified in Basic. If more English speakers would train themselves to lighten the task, the gain in other ways would be immense. More than merely linguistic understanding would be in course of achievement.

To prepare oneself for this costs some trouble—less than may be supposed, as I have argued above, but still some effort. But this is as it should be. The work of making English a universal second tongue should not be all on the learner's side. And only through such out-going effort visibly made in the right spirit can those suspicions and resentments which I began by mentioning be set at rest. Whether they are actually felt abroad, I doubt, but the supranationally-minded English speaker often feels them. They are a reminder, which he will not need, that all the technical apparatus and facilities in the world will be no help to man if he seeks his own first and takes " the general good " to be only the slogan of some pressure group of individuals or nations.

Here, then, for those who are willing and able to cultivate sympathetic co-operations across the language frontiers, is a way of working toward reconstruction. Fifteen years of experiment and test, of development in texts and in reading materials, have provided the means. There is no claim that Basic is perfect. No claims indeed of any sort are needed. These pages are no more than a description of what it is, what it has done, and how it may be used. The hour of the most effective use is soon coming, the hour of reconstruction. It will pass. Hope and resolve will cool. The enterprising spirit will dull down into routine again unless in that hour enough is done to transform the urges of disaster into lasting influences favouring unity. We must act while the lesson lasts. And what the lesson teaches above all else is that the peoples of the earth must know one another better—not through official channels but more directly.

The medium exists. Its period of trial or of tutelage, the need for control and observation, for protection and support, may be taken to be over. What it now needs to go into maximum action is careful use by as many, among its 200 million potential instructors, as have the opportunity, the necessary knowledge, and the ability. A common language for the earth will only come into being through the common work of common men and women in their common interests. Official encouragement from governments, school systems, and other bodies could be a great help. So could the action of powerful individuals. But it is the men and women with the opportunity, knowledge, and ability to aid a beginner in English who will really carry the load. After the war almost anyone may, so far as transport is concerned, go anywhere within a few hours. Opportunity, therefore, will not be lacking. And the necessary knowledge—for anyone who has read this through to the end—will be a matter at most of a few days' diligent study. The rest is good will, imagination, and a belief in mutual understanding.

English of some sort is undoubtedly going to be the chief medium for the wider contacts and co-operations of the air age. People must communicate, and when they are suddenly mixed together in practical undertakings they will use the medium that

is most available. Academic arguments have very little effect
upon what they will in fact do. At countless points on the earth's
surface, English will be the most available language—English
of some sort. The questions then are : How broken need that
English be ? and : How much strain upon those concerned need
these inevitably faulty communications put ? Both are important
—the first for the protection of English, the second for general
amity. I have been attempting to make clear what the uses of
Basic are in these and in other connections.

Appendix

A SELECTION OF BOOKS ON OR IN BASIC ENGLISH

B.E.P.C. = Basic English Publishing Co. 10 King's Parade, Cambridge

Basic English (Kegan Paul). An introduction, with rules and grammar ; containing as Part II a " Short Guide " written in Basic English.

The System of Basic English (Harcourt, Brace). A general account with examples of Basic English, containing, as Part II, *The ABC of Basic English.*

The ABC of Basic English (Kegan Paul). An analysis of the details of the Basic system written in Basic. It has been translated into French, German, Japanese, and some other languages as an adult introduction to Basic (see pp. 49-50).

Basic Step by Step (Kegan Paul). A presentation of the 850 words in associated groups arranged in short descriptive passages annexed to illustrations. Copious notes and teaching suggestions are included which are the basis for numerous adaptations in other languages.

The Basic Words (Kegan Paul). A listing of the recommended uses of the 850 words, their extensions and specializations, with French and German " equivalents " for root senses.

Basic English and Grammatical Reform (B.E.P.C.). By C. K. Ogden. Suggestions for a radical reconstruction of approaches to the teaching of English grammar.

Basic in Teaching : East and West (Kegan Paul). By I. A. Richards. A discussion of the place of Basic in the schools of China and in the English class at home.

Basic by Isotype (Kegan Paul). A brilliantly clear presentation through the international picture language designed by O. Neurath.

The General Basic English Dictionary (Evans). Gives more than 40,000 senses of 20,000 words in Basic English definitions.

Learning the English Language : A Book for Men and Women of All Countries, Books I-III (Houghton Mifflin). A beginners' text graded for class use, with a Teachers' Edition giving full notes on method.

SIMPLER READINGS IN BASIC

Keawe's Bottle (Kegan Paul). R. L. Stevenson's *The Bottle Imp* in Basic.

Mr. Midshipman Easy (B.E.P.C.). A Basic abridgment of Captain Marryat's novel.

Pinocchio (Kegan Paul). By Collodi.

Stories for the Young (Kegan Paul). By Leo Tolstoi.

Stories from China (Kegan Paul). By T. K. Ch'u.

Stories from France (Kegan Paul). By Perrault.

Black Beauty (Kegan Paul). By Anna Sewell.

Japanese Stories (Kegan Paul). By Lafcadio Hearn, with parallel Basic version.

The Gold Insect (Kegan Paul). Poe's *Gold Bug* in Basic.

Gulliver in Lilliput (Kegan Paul). A Basic version of the first part of Swift's *Gulliver's Travels*.

Wise Words of an Early American (Kegan Paul). By Benjamin Franklin.

OUR CHANGING TIMES (B.E.P.C.)

A series of eighteen short books in Basic English about the world in which we live.

Across the Isthmus of Panama	E. Elsbree
All About Motion Pictures	F. W. Wead
Electric Power at Work	M. Haynes
Fireside Stories	M. S. G. Phelan
Great Discoveries	A. C. Perry and G. A. Price
How Men Have Kept Their Records	M. Lipman
Late Night Special	L. J. Hazam
Schoolboys of Early Times (Part I)	B.D. Hurley and I.C. Sartorius
Schoolboys of Early Times (Part II)	*idem*
Ships of Yesterday	L. M. Elholm
The First Virginians	A. Dwight
The Post Bag	E. W. Nolan
The Potter's Wheel	E. Berry
Thunder Bird	W. Evans
To Far Cathay	W. C. Bagley, Jr.
White Man Comes to New York	G. R. Spoerer
Wings Away	J. E. Mooney
Wires Round the Earth	V. Stout

Basic Picture Talks (B.E.P.C.). By L. W. Lockhart. An outline of the connections between the senses of some important words.

FOR MORE ADVANCED READERS

The Three Signs (Kegan Paul). A selection of short stories by Hawthorne, Irving, and Poe.

The Two Friends (Kegan Paul). A story by Tourgenieff.

Arms and the Man (B.E.P.C.). By Bernard Shaw.

Carl and Anna (Kegan Paul). By Leonhard Frank. A Basic version of a sophisticated German novel.

Death in High Society (Kegan Paul). Short stories by Inez Holden.

The Meno of Plato (Kegan Paul). By J. Rantz. In Basic English with notes.

That Night (Kegan Paul). By Tumura. A Japanese play with transliterated Japanese text and two Basic English versions, one literal and one free.

General History (Nelson). By E. H. Carter and C. K. Ogden. The story of man from the earliest times to the present day, viewed from an international angle.

The New Testament in Basic English (Cambridge Press). A new translation under the direction of Professor S. H. Hooke, who holds the Chair of Old Testament Studies in the University of London. (The complete *Basic Bible* will be published in 1944.)

The Republic of Plato (Norton). An abridged version in which use has been made of Basic, by I. A. Richards.

Julius Cæsar (B.E.P.C.) Shakespeare's tragedy with parallel Basic version and notes.

Julius Cæsar (Kegan Paul). A Basic version of selections from the Histories of Julius Cæsar and Brutus in North's Plutarch.

Statement and Suggestion (Kegan Paul). By A. P. Rossiter. A study of the use of Basic in the interpretation of verse.

SCIENCE IN BASIC FOR THE GENERAL READER

European Science (B.E.P.C.). By H. S. Hatfield.

Inventions and their Uses in Science To-day (Pitman). By H. S. Hatfield.

Living Things (Nelson). By J. W. N. Sullivan. An account of the structure of living material and the development of living forms.

The Outlook of Science (Kegan Paul). A selection from the writings of J. B. S. Haldane.

Science and Well-Being (Kegan Paul). A further selection from the writings of J. B. S. Haldane.

What Things Are Made of (B.E.P.C.). By H. S. Hatfield. A short account of the guiding facts of present-day chemistry.

The Growth of Science (Pitman). By A. P. Rossiter. A history of men's theories and discoveries, also published as a Pelican Special in the Penguin Books Series.

Basic for Science (Kegan Paul). A general account of its uses.

Index

ABG of Psychology, 80
Absolutely, 58
Africa, 68, 86
Aims of Basic, 43, 62-71
Analysis, 40
Apperception, 98-99
Aristotle, 5, 99, 103, 105
Attacks on Basic, 28, 33, 45, 49, 56, 61, 63, 94
Australia, 35

Bacon, 5
Basic, and broken English, 44, 64, 120 ; and the deaf, 65 ; and democratic theory, 109-110 ; in English-speaking classes, 94-100, 104-6 ; as fender to English, 6, 16, 29, 47, 120, and public communications, 107-110 ; and public health, 107-8 ; and the rest of English, 46, 115 ; specimens, 21, 24, 41, 42, 98, 109, 110 ; teaching texts, 49 ; verbs, 25, 30, 50-2, 55, 70 ; and visual aids, 80-90 ; Word List, 26-8, 44, 54, 63, 105
Bengali, 17
Bennett, Arnold, 60
Bentham, 10
Bismarck, 20
Boyle, Rudolph, 113-114
Brazil, 35
Bridges, Robert, 47
Broken English, 44, 64, 120

Calendar terms, etc., 34
Cambridge Magazine, 59
Cantonese, 17
Childishness of texts, 78, 91
China, 5, 14, 18, 29, 35, 37, 64, 68, 86, 112, 114
Chinese, 10, 15, 17, 21, 42, 44, 48

Code conception of language, 117
Communications, mental, 5, 36, 89, 120 ; physical, 6, 120
Confucius, 112
Construing, 33, 50, 68
Copyrighting of Basic Word List, 63
Corruption of languages, 16
Crookshank, G., 23
" Cultural imperialism," 14, 119
Czechoslovakia, 38

Danes, 40-1
Denmark, 38, 114
" Difficulty," 77
Difficulty of Basic for English speakers, 101, 113-4, 118
Directives, 29-30, 52-3
Discovery of Basic, 22-4, 42, 47

Empson, W., 37
-er, -ing, -ed endings, 33
Esperanto, 11-13
Evans, E., 38

Fadiman, Clifton, 59
Faraday, 36
Fell, John, 74
Film-loop rivet guns, 83, 88
Foreign languages, 18, 42
French, 16, 17, 42, 92
Frequency, 54, 58, 59
Fries, Charles C. and Traver, A. A., 55
Future of English, 6, 17, 119

Gender, 45, 48
,General Basic English Dictionary, 21, 68, 70, 102, 113
German, 16, 17, 18, 42

Gibson, Christine, 25
Give up, 29, 52
Glaucon, 99, 103
Grading, 72-7
Grammar, 16, 22, 34, 40-42, 48, 67, 74
Greece, 38

Haldane, J. B. S., 36
Hardy, Thomas, 60
Hatfield, H. S., 37
Head words, 28
Hess, Rudolph, 20
History, ignorance of, 91
Horn, Ernest, 54
Humanities, 111

Ido, 11
Illiteracy, 85-7
India, 14, 18, 68, 86
International words, 35
Italian, 16, 17

Japan, 5, 86
Japanese, 17, 38
Jespersen, 41, 74
Johnson, Dr., 29
Joyce, James, 64

Landing stages in learning, 44
Latin, 10, 11, 18, 41, 97
Learning the English Language, 49, 87
Lee, Mr. and Mrs., 107-8
Leibnitz, 23
Leonard, Stirling Andrus, 74
Limitation of words, 43, 60
Limited senses of Basic words, 22, 56
Lin Yutang, 112
Literature, 15, 17, 68
Lockhart, L. W., 23, 44, 82

Madagascar, 11

Massachusetts civic education classes, 76, 87
Margate Royal School for Deaf and Dumb Children, 65
Meaning of Psychology, 80
Measurement terms, etc., 35
" Melting pot " function, 18
Motion-picture teaching, 15, 18, 80-90

Nations, 5, 10
New York Times, 91
Nietzsche, 100
" No verbs," 25
Norman conquest, 41
Novial, 11
Nulango, 11
Numbers, etc., 34

Ogden, C. K., 22-3, 25, 28, 33, 35-6, 45, 52, 54-5, 59-61, 62-3, 66, 80
Olson, Elder, 103
On, 30, 53
Operation words, 24-32, 54, 57-59
Operators, 25
Order in learning, 22, 30, 32, 54, 57, 70, 72, 75-6

Paget, Sir Richard, 45
Payne Fund, 39
Perry, R. B., 109
Plato, 38
Plurals, 43
Plutarch, 38
Populations, 17
Portuguese, 17, 42
Preposition-adverbs, 29-32, 52-4, 80
Pressure groups, 9, 119
Primary languages, 10, 13
Pronouns, 16, 28, 45

Radio, 6, 64, 110
Rantz, J., 38
Rate of learning Basic, 65, 88, 115-6
Reading texts, 36, 91-3

"Real English," 46
Reconstruction, 6, 89, 112
Regularization, 45
Remembering, 80, 83, 88, 115
Reporting, 14
Robinson, T. H., 38
Rockefeller Foundation, 39
Rossiter, A. P., 37, 94
Rulon, P. J., 82
Russia, 16, 17
Russian, 16, 17, 35

Santee, Frederick L., 95
Scholarly and popular words, 40
Science, 36-9
Scott, Sir Walter, 73
Shakespeare, 6, 38, 64, 102
Shall, 72-4
Shaw, 60
Siam, 9
Smith, Edwin S., 38
Smith, Logan Pearsall, 73
South America, 16, 18, 86
Spanish, 15-7, 18, 42
Speech community figures, 17
Spelling, 33, 34, 47
Structure words, 24-32, 54, 57-9
Sullivan, J. W. N., 37
Sweeney, J. L., 94, 107

The Basic Words, 28, 32, 56
" Thinking in English," 117
Thorndike, E. L., 55
Tilley, Winthrop, 94
Translation, 94-98
Transport, mental, 6, 36, 89 ; physical, 14, 119
Traver, A. A., *see* Fries

Unregular, 46
Upton, Albert W., 94
Use and language, 12

Visual aids, 80-90

Walt Disney Studio, 85
Wells, H. G., 60, 113-114
Whitehead, A. N., 103
Wilkins, 23
Will and *shall*, 73-5
Word magic, 23
Word order, 16, 50
Words at Work, 25
World controls, 14

Youth and democracy, 110